Discovering Me

The Journey to Long Gray Hair in a Cut & Dyed World

Connie Sue Cowan

Unless otherwise indicated, all Scripture quotations
are taken from the Holy Bible, New Living Translation,
copyright © 1996, 2004, 2007. Used by permission of
Tyndale House Publishers, Inc. Carol Stream, Illinois
60188. All rights reserved.

For Judy, my sister and biggest supporter. As one who battles chronic hair loss from health conditions she has been my sounding board and encourager as I have walked this journey to long hair. Never judgment, always love. Thank you Judy Ann for prodding me not to give up.

Also greatest thanks to my Two Sister's Retreat gals for the endless prayer support: Lynn, Susan, Cathy, Nan, Hope, Gaye, G.K., Marti, Rosemary, Tanna – I love you all!

'Introduction

I've always wanted to write a book. I toyed with it in the forms of blogs, email devotional messages and numerous journals yet never took the big step to actually attempt putting something cohesive together. In the summer of 2013 I was in the biggest slump of my life, for no discernible reason. With the encouragement of my sister, and with many hours of soul searching, I realized I had a story to tell and it revolved around my hair. Whether it is ever read or not makes no difference, I must write it.

For most men this will probably seem like a silly or insignificant topic, being so concerned with my hair. Perhaps in reading these words from deep in my heart you will understand just a bit of how a woman's mind works (I know, a scary thought)! Women, I think you will recognize yourself in these pages and hopefully start to think about what it is that holds you back and why.

Not too many things throw us into a tizzy quite like the relationship we have with our hair. Millions of dollars are spent on hair products, hours are spent arranging and fixing it 'just so'. When a woman is diagnosed with cancer and faces treatment the first question is rarely about the pain or outcome but it is often "Will I lose my hair!?" We color it, cut it, straighten it, curl it and most of us always want what our own hair is not. We keep those hair stylists in business! Hair is one of those things that is determined by our genetics, yet we try desperately to manipulate it into an expression of whom we want to be, or who we want others to think that we are. There are even religious doctrines that address hair, and what should be done with it.

I don't have particularly memorable hair. My hair is not the much coveted thick, luscious mane that just begs to have hands run through it, though in my mind I keep hoping when I look in the mirror one day God will have miraculously given me just that. Let's

4

just start at my earliest memory of this love/hate relationship with my hair and the deeper story of discovering me.

I have written my story all with the twining thread of 'hair' woven through, but it is really about discovering my Divine Purpose ~ Communicating Freedom. Join me on this journey and perhaps you will uncover some hidden secrets about yourself as well.

1
The Big Chop

At six years old I was finally on my way to that mysterious place called The Beauty Shop. Even at that young age I wondered where it was my mom went every Saturday morning, very early, and would come home transformed. She would carefully comb out her teased and permed hair each Friday night before bed, put a scarf over her head as she left the house the next morning and when she returned home her hair was magically styled. Now I was going there! All of these 51 years later I can still remember Mom parking the car, then walking with her as we entered this mysterious place of odd smells, whirring hair dryers, and women's laughter. Everyone greeted us as we walked in and Beverly said "Connie, are you ready?"

We lived in a very small town in the Sierra foothills of California. One of those towns where everyone knew each other and the local beauty shop was a gathering place for the women, where they checked in with each other and if you listened closely you could hear all of the latest gossip. I loved that town.

Beverly led me to a large swiveling chair that had a board across the arms, a booster seat of sorts. Then she arranged the large, plastic drape around my neck and twirled me around a couple of times. Wow, this was a fun place! No wonder Mom came every week. But soon my excitement at visiting "the beauty shop" turned into total disbelief and sorrow, my first disappointing experience regarding my hair.

You see, I had hair that reached nearly to my waist with just a slight wave to it and an average shade of medium brown. Mom usually fixed it in one long braid down my back, or for a real treat a high ponytail or two braids. I loved how it swished when it was a ponytail day! But all of that was about to change, and I had no idea. I was about to start the first grade and I guess Mom was tired of the daily wrangle to fix my hair. My older sister even got in on the chore sometimes, but I always screamed "Judy is pulling my hair!"

Beverly combed through my long hair and she gathered it all toward the back of my neck. I'm sure I was thinking that she really combed hair nicely, it felt so good. But all of a sudden I saw that she had scissors in her hand......and before I knew it she was holding my precious ponytail in her hand! She reached around and asked "do you want to keep it?" I distinctly remember looking in that large mirror, and seeing Mom standing behind me smiling. But when she saw the tears well up in my eyes and roll down my cheeks I still don't know if she realized what an impact her decision to have my hair cut had made on my tender heart.

Beverly went on to style my hair in a severe pixie cut, very popular for the time, but I hated it. I hid in my room and all of the excitement I was feeling about starting school vanished as I cried because I wouldn't have a ponytail for the first day.

It is interesting how childhood loss affects us. Something as simple as a haircut carries deep emotion for me and I now realize that I have held that feeling in my heart all of these years. This early incident is probably why still to this day I get this little flutter in my heart every time I sit in a stylist's chair and he or she places that drape around me. I wonder subconsciously "is this going to be another drastic change like when I was six years old?" Never underestimate the power of childhood memories. Think about them, ponder them and maybe even spend some time thinking about whether they might have an impact on the strong feelings you experience as an adult.

1 Samuel 16:7 But the Lord said to Samuel, "Do not consider his appearance or his height, for I have rejected him. The Lord does not look at

the things man looks at. Man looks at the
outward appearance, but the Lord looks at the
heart."

1. Take a look at your heart from God's eyes.
What do you carry there from a childhood
experience?

2. Spend some time journaling about a
momentous event from your childhood and how
you respond to it as an adult when you recall
the circumstances. End with a prayer to God
to help you put it in proper perspective
(perhaps you put too little emphasis on its
impact, or perhaps you have pushed it down and
not worked out how it influences you now).

2

Swimming Lessons

Every summer in Jackson, California one of the most exciting things most kids looked forward to was swimming lessons. This celebration of summer was much more than just learning how to master holding your breath, the American crawl or the backstroke; it really was a total experience of Detert Park and the magic that happened there.

I can still picture the concrete blocks of the walls in the dressing room, and struggling to pull that swimming cap on over my hair. In the elementary school years, my hair was growing out from the severe pixie cut and getting all of that unruly hair into a swimming cap was always a challenge. In those days girls weren't allowed in the pool unless a cap was worn. Part of the transition to summer was getting a new swimsuit and picking out a cap that matched. The rubbery smell was the strongest when the cap was removed from the package for the first time. You could always tell which girls had really long hair because their caps would have a telltale bulge in the back from their ponytail. I usually just had stray strands of hair peeking out around the edges of my cap. I was always envious that the boys didn't have to struggle with the cap.

I've mentioned before that this was a small town; all during my childhood the population was probably about 2,500. Directly next to the pool was the Scout Hut. I have no idea who ran this program, but part of the fun of swimming lessons was the summer program that was going on at the Scout Hut. While each age group waited for their lesson, the boys and girls would be hanging out at "the hut". Inside was a magical place! Each summer we would have the most wonderful things to do: ceramic plaster casts to paint, a tooled leather coin purse, plastic lace key chains to make, or one of my favorites: jumping on the trampoline! (This last one gives this Grammy's

12

heart a bit of anxiety, no jumping on trampolines for my granddaughters!) I have never asked or known who ran this summer program, I just know that summers in Jackson at Detert Park were great. I can still remember picking out a set of plaster fruit and painting them beautifully, knowing that my Mom would LOVE them for her kitchen!

Though we were there for swimming lessons, the whole experience of the pool was a myriad of delights. I remember the ice cold water as we all jumped in and had to do bobs to warm up, the seemingly endless laps of different strokes as we practiced our skills. Then going back to that cinder block changing room, finally being able to take that rubber cap off my head and hearing my Mom's voice saying "make sure you put your cap in your bag to bring it home!" You see, I usually needed a replacement cap several times through the summer because I would forget my cap after lessons. There was always a lost and found box at the entrance of the pool, but I never seemed to be able to find my lost caps. If Mom went to buy me another cap she would just get the first thing she saw on the shelf, so sometimes it didn't match my swimsuit, which even then was a traumatic experience.

This great pool was the sparkling jewel at the city park. I have great memories at all stages about this park. Each area of the park was the gathering place for different age groups. There was the playground that also led down to the creek - the boys usually hung out there. There was a wooded area where we would pretend that we were in a great forest and chase each other around with games of tag or hide-and-seek. The older kids and teens were in the sunnier areas of the park, always working on their tans with bottles of baby oil, iodine and a transistor radio playing the latest hits. There was also a road circling the perimeter of the park, and teen boys would be cruising to see if the girl of their dreams was sunbathing, or they would park and wax their cars in preparation for a date with the girls they spotted in the park. In the evenings, the upper half of the park was the place to be for Little League games or slow pitch softball. I remember watching all of the different groups of kids and dreaming about when I would be old enough to lay my beach towel out on the lawn and get the perfect tan (on my breaks from being a lifeguard, of course).

Another highlight of summers at Detert Park was the afternoon breaks during swimming hours. Each hour the lifeguards would blow their whistle for a 10-minute break in the 2:00pm to 5:00pm swimming hours of the afternoon. The local Safeway grocery store was just down the hill, so we would wrap up in our towels and put our rubber thongs on our feet and slosh into the store for a Popsicle or candy bar.

There are so many things about my childhood in a small town that just don't exist anymore. My heart grieves that children today aren't able to be dropped off at the local pool, take swimming lessons and freely walk across the lot to the Scout Hut for fun arts, crafts and recreation. I'm sure there were competent adults in charge and there was an organized program in place, but all I remember is that it was fun, I was with my friends, my parents weren't there and I got to make cool stuff to take home. Yes, I learned how to swim. I couldn't wait to promote from the pollywog class and go to the 'big pool'. Every summer there was no question how time would be spent once school was out – it was swimming lessons and afternoons at the pool. Looking back what I really learned over those summers was that being with friends was fun, that I really could put my hair in a swim cap, and, with a ring of people around the edge for safety, jumping on a trampoline was super fun! I also got the first inkling of my driven personality and wanting to be in charge. I knew early on that I wanted to be a lifeguard so I could blow that whistle and tell other people what to do.

Proverbs 22:6 Train a child in the way he should go, and when he is old he will not turn from it.

1. Looking back on your childhood what lessons did you learn that you now recognize were the first indications of your personality?

2. If you could pass on a favorite experience from your childhood to a child today what would it be?

3. Write a prayer to God asking for help in recapturing your childhood dreams and blending that into who you are today. Begin the journey of discovering the 'you' that has been inside since you were young.

I know not everyone has fond childhood memories like I do. If you had a difficult childhood and choose not to return to that place, ask God to reveal to you a release from

the pain of those memories and move closer to
peace with Him.

3

Juice Cans and Hairspray

My only sister is eight years older than me, and I have looked up to her all of my life. I remember sitting in the evenings and watching her roll her hair on juice cans so that she would have the perfect large curl. After what I'm sure was a sleepless night on those hard cans she would then tease the heck out of her hair and fog the room with hairspray as she would achieve the perfect flip or page boy style before going off to school. I'm so thankful that eight years later when I was in high school the look of the day was long hair, parted in the middle. Though I did give the juice can rollers a try, no hair spray for me!

Long hair became an important thing in the high school years. Though I was always vocal in how I wanted my hair to look through elementary school after the traumatic big chop, once I got to high school I just settled for several years of long, fairly straight but nice hair. Most of my friends wore their hair in a similar style; just one glance through a 1970's era yearbook will show you that. So how did my leadership personality start to develop in the midst of this environment where we all looked and dressed the same? Though I didn't recognize it at the time, as I look back I can see that I sought out leadership roles and was never afraid to speak my mind or be in front of people. I was outspoken and didn't mind taking chances. What most people didn't know is that I was so insecure inside and needed those public accolades because I never really believed I was good at anything. I perfected the art of being very self-assured in public but would agonize in private over my shortcomings. I always felt not quite good enough.

Going back to my analogy of hair, what is it that we are doing when we women roll our hair on juice cans, use curling irons, or like I remember my sister's friends doing: ironing hair with a clothes iron? We are trying to make our hair do what we want it to do. I have two granddaughters that have wildly different hair. The oldest one has basically straight hair like her mother, nice and thick and it perfectly suits her. The younger one, as I write this she is 19 months old, and she has this fabulous super curly hair like her daddy's. Not long ago my daughter and I were talking as we watched the girls play. I commented to her that I hope she realizes that she is going to have the ultimate battle with these two girls. I can hear it now: "Mom, I want a perm so my hair is like Ryleigh's!" Or – "Why does my hair have to be so curly and thick, Mom please straighten my hair so it looks like Chloe's". Perhaps these two girls will break the mold and actually love the hair they have, but I'm not holding my breath on that one!

What is it inside of us that makes us want so badly to be something we are not? Most of us fight against the wonderful aspects of ourselves. I don't know of many young people that truly appreciate who they are and I guess that is why when we get to be more mature (old!) we wish we could impart what we have learned to those who struggle so much. But that is the nature of life, isn't it? We bumble through the years, making decisions and hopefully somewhere along the way we discover who we really are and grow into that. This book is my journey to that very place. It took a summer of depression and self-reflection to move me forward. I have had a basically good life yet there is this yearning inside of me for more. To reach the age of 57 and feel like I have been living someone else's life is a real show stopper. I woke up one day and realized that I didn't want to be molded by juice can rollers, or held in place by restrictive hair spray - making me appear to others to be someone I'm not. When we step outside into humid air, a rain storm or high wind, the carefully crafted look we have achieved with those rollers and hairspray suddenly collapses and we are vulnerable and exposed. My deepest desire is to be real, all of the time, but it has taken me a long time to get to this spot.

Psalm 139:14 I praise you because I am fearfully and wonderfully made; your works are wonderful, I know full well.

1.   **Express your thoughts about being "fearfully and wonderfully made" and your acceptance of how God created you.**

2.   **What hinders you from accepting yourself as you are?**

3.   **What are the hidden parts of your being that God placed inside of you that you wish others could see?**

4.   **Write a prayer asking God's help in being the 'real you' - for all to see.**

4

A Hop, Skip and a LEAP!

1970 was a memorable year for me. I was in the 7th/8th grade that year and for the most part it was carefree. My sister was already married and out of the house, so I enjoyed my 'only child' status. She would tell you that I was terribly spoiled and got away with way more than she ever did!

Though our family was not necessarily regular church attenders, my parents always dropped me off for Sunday School and worship, and they also knew that I wanted to participate in every event the youth group had planned. One such event was a turning point for my entire life. The wonderful couple that were our youth sponsors had planned a day trip to hear a speaker at a revival. Though I had no idea what a revival was, I was ready to go on a road trip. Any time we left our little hometown and went to the big city was a special occasion. It turned out that this

24

event was to hear David Wilkerson and Nicky Cruz speak. You may know that David Wilkerson was the author of The Cross and the Switchblade, his personal account of ministering to gang members, and Nicky Cruz was one of his converts.

As I listened to these men speak, hearing stories of gang violence, drugs and things that were so far removed from my small-town experience, my heart was greatly moved by the salvation story. I remember still to this day thinking "If God can change people like these violent, murdering gang members, then surely He loves me too". I was one of the teens in our group that responded to the altar call that day. At age 13, in a football stadium in Stockton, California, I gave my life to Jesus. Little did I know how this would change everything! At age 57, I am still learning and uncovering how deeply and truly God loves me. What started as I kneeled before God at age 13 is still working its way deep into my soul, and this book is one way that I am coming to accept that unconditional love from God.

Upon returning home after the revival, we of course were chatterboxes on the hour-long drive back to the church. I started reading my Bible every chance I got, and I even took it to school with me. My friends, including the ones who had also attended the revival, thought I had lost my mind. While they too had enjoyed the experience, I don't recall that any of them came back determined to 'save' all of our heathen friends like I did! Of course, my enthusiasm waned as I had little skill in sharing the newfound Gospel with my other classmates, but I did continue to read my Bible and knew that God wanted more from me. I also didn't have a dramatic story like those former gang members, so I really never thought anyone would listen to me talk about Jesus and how much he loves us.

Looking back now I realize this is the start of me pushing down the desire to lead and teach about God. It was bubbling inside of me, but I had no direction in how to nurture it. Later in life this passion would come out in many ways, but I will get to that in later chapters.

The only hair analogy I can bring to this chapter is that I think the wandering feeling that I felt during my early teen years is when I first felt like pulling my hair out in frustration, or simply pulling it back in a ponytail because I didn't want to mess with it. Like my budding Christianity, it was easier to have things out of sight rather than address them or fuss with them. But God has a way of always bringing us back to Him.

Romans 10:9-10 That if you confess with your mouth, "Jesus is Lord", and believe in your heart that God raised him from the dead, you will be saved. For it is with your heart that you believe and are justified, and it is with your mouth that you confess and are saved.

1. Recount a time in your life when you have had the realization that there is something bigger than you, and that perhaps it is God calling out to you for a relationship with Him.

2. If you have had that defining moment of being saved by God for eternal life with Him, write about how you felt. If you have not yet had that life-changing experience, write your thoughts about how you feel about faith, God and what a relationship with Him might mean to you.

3. What is your biggest challenge in pursuing a life of faith, or deepening your current relationship with God?

*If you do not have a church home, ask friends about a Bible believing/teaching place of worship in your area. Pray for God to lead you to someone who will walk with you on your faith journey. You may also write or email me; I would love to talk more in depth about your desire to accept Christ into your life.

5

Tickling the Ivories

Though no one in my immediate family was particularly musically gifted, we always had music of some sort playing in our home. I remember fondly when my mom would put her Nat King Cole albums on the record player, or sometimes it was Glenn Miller and other Big Band sounds. Saturday afternoons (after her start at the Beauty Shop) always meant Hee Haw on the television, followed by other country music shows while she did her weekly laundry and ironing.

At some point I decided I wanted to play the piano. My parents found a used piano from someone in town, and they set out to find me a teacher. The first time I walked into Mrs. Duff's living room I knew it was going to be a special place. Her walls were lined with publicity photos of her in jazzy costumes, dancing or playing the piano with the likes of Louis Armstrong. Those photos told a story of her earlier life and even though they were all black and white glossy 8X10s, I could just imagine myself at every event. Those years were far behind her, and though I never knew how she wound up in a tiny town in the Sierra foothills of California, I was so excited to have Mrs. Duff as my piano teacher.

Though she was probably in her 60s by the time she was teaching me, she was still quite active in our small community. Not only was she the most sought-after piano teacher, she also played accompaniment for local events with the most fascinating being background sound effects on the organ for the county fair rodeo! Her living room was dominated by a beautiful baby grand piano, as well as a large organ. She could sit down and play wonderful music "by ear", but early on in the first years of my lessons I discovered that all of her students were expected to warm up with Hannon finger exercises, then master many classical pieces through hours of practice. I can still see those pale yellow music books propped up on my piano. I wanted to rush ahead and learn jazz, or popular music, but she insisted on correctly performing classical music first.

After several years of taking lessons, in the spring when I was 14 years old it was again recital time. I was finally going to play a substantial piece by Bach, from memory. If I recall correctly it was about 10 pages long, and I knew I could do it. But the most exciting thing about that recital was my hair! A trip was planned to that same dreaded beauty shop, but this time for my first up-do. I had cut out pictures and I knew I wanted a head full of ringlet curls cascading down my back, especially since most of the audience would be looking at my back as I sat at the piano; I wanted it to be a nice view.

I can't remember how I performed that night, but I sure remember how I felt walking out of that salon with a fancy hairdo. It was firmly fixed in place with lots of hairspray and numerous bobby pins, and I felt like a

32

princess. This time Beverly got it right with my picture in hand and me speaking my mind, the outcome was much better than the big chop when I was 6. I have had many up-dos since that time, but I don't think any of them have been as special as that first one. To be transformed into someone else for a night, simply by changing my hair, was a magical feeling. I walked different, sat straighter, and I KNOW I played the piano better – all because I had a fancy hairstyle, patterned after one of those glossy photos I had seen in my piano teacher's living room.

It was also my first realization that I am not one of those people who gets nervous in front of others. I thrive on it. I never became a great piano player, though I can still play for my own enjoyment. I rarely played in front of others after those years of lessons, but I love walking out on a stage or up to a microphone to speak. That big recital was also about a year after my conversion experience at the revival. I had talked with

Mrs. Duff about that experience and she was one of the few adults who knew how deeply I was moved by that event. She even let me stray a bit from my classical pieces and helped me learn a beautiful arrangement of How Great Thou Art that was my second piece for that recital. That great hymn became an expression of what was in my heart. I still get very emotional when I hear or sing it.

Fancy hair, a beautiful white dress with tiny black pin dots, and a recital hall filled with family and friends made for a memorable evening. I can picture it all in my mind all these years later, but what resonates the most are the words of that hymn: *"then sings my soul, my Savior God to thee, how great thou art, how great thou art"*. God was calling out to me, but I was about to start many years of running in the opposite direction.

Psalm 100:2 Worship the Lord with gladness; come before him with joyful songs.

1. What hobbies or special activities did you participate in as a child or teen? What did you learn about yourself in those activities?

2. Write a bit about an adult who had a special influence in your life when you were young; what about that person helped you discover something about yourself?

3. What music do you remember from childhood, and what types of memories does that music invoke when you hear it?

4. How might you be an influence to a young person today? Will you act on it?

6

Cheers!

The years 1972-75 were some fun ones. I talk to many people who struggled through high school, but I loved those years. I had a great group of girlfriends to share those times with. With little effort I was able to maintain a high grade point average and I was discovering more every year that I loved being in charge or in front of people.

I sought out leadership roles, class offices and club committees. The activity I loved the most was cheerleading. I had been a cheerleader in the seventh and eighth grades, but high school was the 'big time'! I was determined to try out for yell leader (that is what the position was called at that time) at the end of my freshman year. During those years, there didn't seem to be the giant squad of gymnastics athletes who make up the cheer teams these days. The yell leaders did just that; they led the fans in yells and cheers for the home team. There were only three members on the yell squad and six on the song leader team. The song leaders were the girls who did great routines along with the band, and they used pom-poms. I was all about the yelling, no song leader position for me!

I prepared, practiced and made my giant campaign posters for the yell leader tryouts. I passed out flyers and decided on a high ponytail with a large white bow for my hair that day. All of the hopefuls had gone through a couple of weeks of practice to learn the routine. For the tryouts we were expected to do one group cheer, and one cheer on our own. There were only four of us trying out, and one was a boy. I was the only freshman trying out, so I knew it was a long shot. At the end of the day when the results were read, I had lost out to the boy. I was so crushed! It was kind of a novelty to have a boy on the squad, but he would be able to do lifts and jumps, propelling us to a new status in the county league at football games that next fall.

Cheer camp was held at Squaw Valley Resort in northern California shortly after school got out. I was so envious when the newly picked squad was headed out for the week-long camp to learn new cheers for the upcoming school year. Being a small town, there was always a sendoff when the cheer and song squads left for camp. About a week later I got the biggest surprise of my life. The cheer advisor called me and said the boy who had won decided it wasn't for him, and he quit - I was in! Though I had missed out on the camp experience, I hit the ground running that summer and learned all of the cheers; I was so excited to be part of the Jackson Pep Squad.

Over the next three years of high school I stayed very involved in the pep squad and I continued to notice my pattern of wanting to be in charge. By my senior year I knew I wanted to be Head Cheerleader, and I set out to achieve that. You see, the Head

Cheerleader was not only one who called the cheers that were to be led, this person also served as the president, of sorts, over the whole squad. This consisted of the three cheerleaders, six song leaders and the two school mascots. So I got to lead the squad meetings, I was the go between for the faculty and squad members and I got to yell! What could be better?

This was also my first taste of leadership, carrying responsibility and accountability. During our senior year we had a great boys basketball team. I recall during one particularly heated and close game there was a bad call, in my opinion, against our team. I promptly started a rather degrading cheer, which the fans took up fervently: "Get a rope, get a tree, and we'll hang the referee"…..this was repeated many times, each time getting louder and louder until I heard that shrill sound of the referee's whistle – FOUL! We had a technical called on the crowd, and it was under my leading. Needless to say

I had a session in the principal's office the next morning. I can't remember the outcome of that particular game, but I certainly never forgot the lesson. In a leadership position, I had great influence and sometimes it could be used in hurtful ways.

As I was writing this chapter, I stopped to take a glance through my old yearbooks. I did a quick count of my class and, of the 24 girls in the class, 20 of us wore our hair parted (usually in the middle), long and straight. It was the look of the times. Though all of us were quite different, you really couldn't tell it by our hair. As cheerleaders we would decide before each game whether to wear our hair down, up in a ponytail, white bow, green bow, half up half down, but always we would wear it the same. As I was discovering more and more that I wanted to stand out and be noticed, I still went along with the crowd and when it came to hair I was right there with the rest. The struggle was trying to fit in while still shining in my own right, and it was hard at times.

There was also a dangerous pattern emerging during my high school years. While I was leading cheers all during the school year, I was also discovering alcohol. My closest girlfriends and I spent a lot of time together, and after games we usually stayed at one another's homes for the night. None of them were on the pep squad, so all the party arrangements would be made by them, and I would be my perky self at games, then off to party afterward. We started experimenting with blender drinks, daiquiris being one of our favorites. I don't like to think of the choices we made back then, and I'm thankful that none of us had severe consequences or got hurt. I could probably write an entire book just on some of the stupid things we did. The hardest part of all of this for me was the struggle going on inside. Kind of like my long hair, parted in the middle just like everyone else, I put on a happy face and went with the crowd. Inside I kept feeling something wasn't quite right; there was a gnawing at my heart I didn't understand. I would write in my diary, and those writings would usually take the form of prayers. God was still part of my life, but I kept Him boxed up and in private. I talked to Him and wondered about some of the choices I was making, but I never got any clear answers, mostly because I wasn't listening.

I also was starting to notice the nasty path that alcohol can lead to. My parents had always been social drinkers. Their young adult life was the time of cocktail parties and card games. By the time I was in high school my dad's business was failing, he was working various jobs to make ends meet and he was spending more time at the local bar than at home. It was a troubling thing and took its toll on all of us. There was no violence or abuse, just the dad I loved sinking into despair and failure. I hated seeing him drunk, and I was learning that alcohol has a way of creeping into lives and I didn't want it ruining mine, yet I still drank with my friends.

Being in front of a cheering crowd made me happy. I loved the excitement and the energy of all of us united in supporting our guys in whatever sport was being played. I was learning that leadership is fun, and it is more about being part of something bigger than me. I was finding that desire to ignite passion in others and get them excited, mostly in good ways. But I also remember teaching some younger schoolmates how to mix a blender drink, so leadership can be used in negative ways too. Whether it is leading a derogatory cheer before a frenzied crowd, or introducing a young impressionable girl who looks up to the 'head cheerleader' how to drink alcohol; with leadership comes responsibility. God was still trying to get my attention, but more twists and turns would come before I would turn His way.

Hebrews 10:23-24 Let us hold unswervingly to the hope we profess, for he who promised is faithful. And let us consider how we may spur one another on toward love and good deeds.

1. In what ways do you go along with the crowd? Are you happy doing that, or do you feel an urging to step out on your own path?

2. How do you use your influence with others in positive ways? In negative ways? What do you need to do to make the positive influences outnumber the negative?

3. What action would you like to turn away from right now in order to have more peace within yourself? Ask someone to be your accountability partner in this growth step.

7

Working for the Weekends

In the fall of 1975 my world changed. Most of my friends were leaving for college; I was setting off to attend a trade school. I would be in class for nine months to learn the trade of veterinary assistant. Early on in childhood I had dreamed of being a nurse, but after a stint as an Auxiliary candy striper at our local hospital I knew nursing wasn't going to be for me. So during my senior year I worked part time at a local vet office and decided to pursue being a vet tech.

California had recently implemented the need for licensure for this career field, and after completing the course I would take the test and go to work. Though my heart's desire was to attend "real" college, my parents gently persuaded me to attend a trade school. I didn't learn until much later that they were struggling with money issues and didn't want to go in debt for college. They also didn't want me to start off in debt with student loans. The idea of university was just kind of skipped over and I went to trade school. Later in life I came to realize this was just the first of many instances where I went along with the flow, being a good girl and not pursuing options for myself.

That next year I secured my first job as a vet tech in Redding, California. I did love the work, but I had my first experience of gender discrimination. I worked in a large vet hospital, and the lead doctor had always had a male vet tech. Even though I was trained and licensed, I basically cleaned the kennels, fed the animals and that was it. No assisting in surgery, or lab procedures that I had been trained to do. I lasted about six months.

My mom was a hard worker. After leaving the family business (in order to bring in more income) my mom worked as an escrow officer at a title company in our home town. I remember as a child telling her "I will never be a secretary" and she would graciously reply "never say never". In the years right after high school I learned firsthand that she was much more than a secretary. As lead escrow officer, she had a lot of responsibility and was excellent at her job, and her employers valued her. She actually got me a job with the title company as I was attending school, before I went to work at the vet office.

I learned a lot at the title company job, as mom was harder on me than most. She didn't want there to be any question of favoritism with her daughter in the office! I learned from the best. So when I quit the veterinary job in Redding I sought out what I knew – I went to work at a title company again. These were pretty good years, and I was enjoying the working world. I was far away from my high school friends, so I didn't think too much about how much fun they were probably having. While my friends were probably wearing jeans to school and still wearing their hair long and carefree, I had moved on to business suits, dresses and wearing my hair in my first curly perm.

A couple of years into this stage of my life I really started pondering what my future would be. I had broken off a relationship with a longtime high school boyfriend. Though we had a great relationship and I think he wanted to move toward settling down, I knew that wasn't for me. Some of my other friends were starting to get engaged, and it seemed so far out of my reach that I just wondered how my life would go.

I had a pretty regular weekly routine. I lived alone in a nice apartment, just me and my parakeet. I worked hard in a large office, had some close girlfriends and generally life was good. But I was pretty obsessed with partying and casual relationships. One of my regular weekly events was to go to the local Holiday Inn for ladies night. The lounge there had a great band, there were always visiting convention attendees looking for a good time, and I LOVED to dance. My

48

girlfriend and I went every Wednesday night, we drank too much, danced a lot and I usually didn't feel too good on Thursday at work. Again, alcohol was having a negative influence in my life.

Each week as time went on I questioned my life path. I still prayed regularly, wrote in my diary daily, usually crying out to God, but I didn't attend church and my private life was such a contrast to my public one. Even my family members didn't know how much I craved a deep relationship with the Jesus I met in that college stadium. I didn't think anyone would believe me, seeing how I was living my life.

At the time, my sister and her family lived about 2 hours away from me in southern Oregon. I used to go see her several weekends a month. That drive through the mountains was the best! I have always loved the mountains and I feel most peaceful in that setting. I had a wonderful Golden Retriever by this time, and Digger would sit in the car next to me as we drove to see Judy. On my many visits I soon met some of the young airmen on the Air Force base where Judy's husband was stationed. A new spark ignited in me and I decided to change my life path completely and enlist in the Air Force.

This was such a drastic step, but when I met with the recruiter I learned that I would have college paid for and I could potentially travel to distant parts of the world. It all sounded very exciting. Both of my parents had served in the military during WWII, Mom in the Marines, and Dad in the Navy. So it wasn't such a foreign idea to enlist. When I told the family they all gave their full support, though surprised since I had never given any indication of this in the past.

From when I made the decision in August of 1979 until October 1979, when I actually left for basic training, my world was a whirlwind of goodbye parties, getting my furniture and belongings disbursed and, sadly, finding a home for my dog. I had moments of wondering what in the world I had done, but I knew my carefree, long hair days were gone and so was my business suit and styled-hair routine; days of uniforms were coming!

Colossians 3:23 Whatever you do, work at it with all your heart, as working for the Lord, not for men.

1. **What kinds of jobs have you had in your life, and how did you approach them? Write a bit about the impact your jobs have had on your life.**

2. **How has your adult life turned out compared to what you envisioned when you were a child or teen? Are you following your dreams?**

3. **What goals do you have for the rest of your life?**

8

Cancer and Wings

As the date approached for me to report for Basic Training at Lackland AFB in San Antonio, Texas, a major bump in the road rose up. My parents asked me to sit with them, and they told me the worst news I had ever received: at age 58, Dad had been diagnosed with lung cancer. I immediately wanted to cancel my enlistment, and my recruiter told me that I could do that, but my dad insisted that I go through with my plans. He told me that I couldn't live my life on "mights" so as hard as it was, I reported to the Oakland, California, recruiting station and said goodbye to my parents. I was starting on a new journey, and I really had no idea what it would bring.

Before leaving I had made one more trip to the beauty shop and had my hair cut. I could have left it long, but I figured with the rigorous schedule of basic training I would conform to uniform standard and cut my hair above the collar. It was a hard thing to do, but I was so glad I had when a few weeks later I only had 5 minutes to roll out of bed, brush teeth and be in formation three flights of stairs down!

Just a few days into training I was realizing that at the age of 22 I was OLD compared to most in the flight. In my usual fashion I pursued leadership and was named a squad leader that first week. Along with that came responsibility and extra duty hours, but I was enjoying it. That is until I came down with a nasty head cold. You can't imagine how frustrating it is to have to blow your nose while in formation but first holler "permission to blow nose? Sir, yes sir!" Also in the midst of the fall of 1979, the Shaw of Iran had been brought to Lackland and the base was on full lock down. As we would be out marching in formation we could see the many news trucks lined up outside of the base gates, but all we were told was that there was an international situation going on, and things were 'fragile'. Soon I again doubted my decision to join. I had had a good job, my own apartment, lots of friends, LONG hair, and on top of all of it my dad was going through cancer treatments. I had quite the pity party in those weeks.

Basic training flew by, and our squad finished in early December. I was able to go home for Christmas after receiving orders for my advanced training that would take place right after the holiday break. I would be reporting to Chanute AFB in Champagne, Illinois, to learn the trade of working on the environmental systems on very large cargo airplanes. I was very excited, and knew that I would go to some exciting places once I finished my technical training.   When   I arrived home I was shocked to see a shell of my dad. He had lost a lot of weight in the eight weeks I had been away, and though feeling okay he didn't look like this was something he would recover from. At the time

54

I had no idea that Christmas of 1979 would be the last time I would see my dad.

My wings of the future were starting to sprout. I knew that I would be living in some faraway place; I knew that I would have an exciting future, but to leave home once again, and say goodbye to the most wonderful man in my life, was heartbreaking. I often wonder what more we could have done together those few holiday weeks I was home, and if I had only known when I said goodbye that it would be the last time, I know I would have held on a little tighter and a little longer. Christmas was a special time for Dad and me; I was always his helper in putting up lights. He was actually pretty obsessive compulsive about how it was done, and I have carried that tradition on (much to my husband's dismay!) I will forever remember standing by the ladder and handing him the strings of lights all those years I was growing up, along with fishing trips, BBQ's, and extra special birthday bouquets delivered to school. There are so many things that I remember about my dad. Flying off to my future, I now think it was probably easier that I would be far away; it would have been way too painful to be home and not see him. Victor Lloyd Koplin is still missed, all of these 35 years later.

Jeremiah 29:11-13 "For I know the plans I have for you," says the Lord. "They are plans for a future and a hope. In those days when you pray I will listen. If you look for me wholeheartedly you will find me."

1. **Have you ever made plans that were completely out of your comfort zone, and possibly even changed the course of your life? How did you move to make those plans and what was the outcome?**

2. **How did you go through the decision making process? Was God a part of your process?**

3. What unexpected events have occurred in your life that have caused you to question your decisions? How do you react to those events?

4. Looking forward, how could you change your decision making process in life decisions?

9
North to the Future

Just a few short months after the death of my dad, I had orders in hand after completing my technical school training with the Air Force. After a long winter in Illinois, learning the trade of Environmental Systems, I was trained to work on large cargo aircraft. My first duty assignment was Elmendorf AFB in Anchorage, Alaska. "North to the Future" is the Alaska state motto and seemed so appropriate for my life.

After a few weeks home on leave following trade school, I arrived in Anchorage on Memorial Day weekend in 1980. My sponsor picked me up and, after some initial in-processing at the base, I was dropped off at what was to be my new home for the next two years. A beautiful red brick multi-story building rose above me, and my room was on the first floor. Due to the fact there were very few women in the aircraft maintenance field at that time, we had one wing of the dorm building to ourselves, and most of us were not assigned a roommate. The most exciting thing, when I first walked up, was the number of young men and women outside playing football and Frisbee on the dorm lawn. It was nearly 10 p.m. and still broad daylight! Summers in Alaska are absolutely beautiful.

As my hair grew out from the severe cut before Basic Training, I was happy to be letting it grow once again. I can still remember the air blowing in my permed curls and the feeling of acceptance as the group outside invited me to join them. I made fast friends there and I can still say that those two years in Alaska are some of my fondest memories. The freedom of growing my hair out again made me feel like myself. I could put it all up in a cap for work and have it loose and casual when off duty.

My future was stretched out ahead of me, and as I settled into the routine of three-day shift rotations of twelve hours on, twelve hours off, I loved the military life more each day. The base sits in the middle of the Alaskan forest, with several lakes on the base property. We would hike, fish, camp and just generally enjoy the outdoors. As summer turned to winter, and everything was covered with snow and ice, I still loved it. Working on the flight line was an adventure at 20 below temps, but with proper clothing and lots of good friends we worked hard and played hard all of the time. I will tell you, there is nothing like catching your first King Salmon; it's exhilarating!

Work hard, play hard was my life then. I had little responsibility, other than my duty hours. I did fall rather quickly into a romantic relationship, so my time was spent with a young man whom I thought was also 'my future'. We ended up going our separate ways when we both left Alaska, but while there I was in even more turmoil as far as God was concerned. I was starting to feel a tug to make the Air Force my career, yet this young man I thought I wanted to spend my life with was returning to civilian life. I would have another two-year duty station to serve before I had to make an enlistment decision; changes yet again were troubling me. I look now at those years and how my faith life was kept mostly in the background, as it had been for the previous few years, but God kept trying to draw me in. I can see my desire to be close to Him was there when I read over my diaries from that time.

Lots of changes came, but little did I know that when I received my duty orders for Laughlin AFB in Del Rio, Texas, my life would change in the biggest way ever.

Proverbs 3:5-6 Trust in the Lord with all your heart; do not depend on your own understanding. Seek his will in all you do and he will show you which path to take.

1. When you think about your future, what excites you?

2. Can you imagine going off in a completely different direction than what is normal for you? What would that look like?

3. What areas do feel God pulling you toward that you have been ignoring? What is holding you back?

4. Journal for yourself, or share with a trusted friend, the things that keep you from stepping out in faith. How would turning those things over to God be different or hard for you?

10

Where Have All The Flowers Gone?

May in Alaska is at the end of "thaw" season. The mud turns to vibrant green and with the long daylight hours the flora and fauna of the area are exquisite. When I left Anchorage, I traveled home to California to enjoy a couple of weeks with family, so I spent time in the beautiful Sierra foothills in spring. Lots of changes were coming as I purchased a car and planned a two-week driving trip across the southwest to wind my way to Del Rio, Texas.

I was scheduled to arrive on Memorial Day weekend, just like my arrival time in Alaska. One of my closest childhood friends made the drive with me and we had great adventures visiting places like the Grand Canyon, Carlsbad Caverns, the Painted Desert and more. One of the most exciting aspects of the trip was how much stuff was loaded in my little hatchback Datsun. We would unload it most nights and lay the seats down so we could sleep in the car at campgrounds! We did run into rain and some shady looking characters at a couple of the planned stops; on those nights we called home and got permission to use our parents' credit cards to get a hotel room for the night.

As we got closer to Texas, we decided to make a circuit route through the state before I had to report for duty. We stopped in Abilene to see some friends I had made at tech school, then on to the Fort Worth/Dallas area. We then traveled south to the area north of Houston called The Woodlands. My friend had made arrangements with some relatives there for us to stay a night. When we drove into The Woodlands I thought it was beautiful; all of the wildflowers and wooded area were so different than most of Texas that we had driven through. I was amazed at the layout of the area, and it was just being settled at that time as a planned community. Little did

I know that just a few years later I would be very familiar with The Woodlands!

We had some fun times in Houston, particularly our visit to Gilley's, where we wanted to see the mechanical bull that had become famous the year before in the hit John Travolta movie "Urban Cowboy". I was feeling that Texas was going to be a fun place. As we continued on our travels, I took my friend to San Antonio and showed her the Riverwalk I had visited while in basic training in 1979. After putting her on the plane back to California, I drove the last 160 miles of my trip across Texas to find my new home.

As I drove farther west, toward the Mexico border I noticed the land was getting flatter, the trees fewer and cactus more numerous. The ground was a dusty white that I later learned was caliche, and when just a few miles from Del Rio I passed the sign that said "Laughlin AFB" – I had arrived. As I entered that base front gate I cried for the first time about reaching my duty station. Every other place I had been so far was exciting and beautiful. I was starting to question whether this military thing was really for me. After the beauty of Alaska and the great trip to arrive there, the desolation I felt at arriving in Del Rio was immense. It looked nothing like the publicity brochures I had received in my welcome packet, and my sponsor was out of town for the Memorial Day weekend so I had to find my own way to the dorm. A far cry from the brick building I had lived in at Elmendorf, my room was in a 1960s era wooden dorm building, with a small room to share with another young woman. That first night I was introduced to GIANT palmetto water bugs, (the biggest roaches you will ever see!) and the loneliest night I ever remember in my life. I definitely wasn't in Alaska anymore.

I learned very quickly to wear my hair in a high ponytail, anything to keep it up and away in the oppressive heat, even in late May. No Frisbee or football when I arrived, just a small base and very few people around. I still had no idea how much this town would mean in my life; all I longed for was to be back in the mountains and to see the lush green woods and beautiful flowers of summer in Alaska. 'God, where have all my flowers gone?' I thought.

Ecclesiastes 3:1 There is a time for everything, and a season for every activity under heaven.

1. **Recall a time in your life when things seemed to be going against you in every way. Looking back, what did you learn during that time?**

2. **What is your attitude toward God when things aren't going the way you plan or desire?**

3. **How can difficult times in your past help you going forward?**

4. What advice would you give to someone else when things aren't going their way?

11

"I do"

I quickly settled into a new routine that was much different from my previous duty station. When assigned to the Military Airlift Command squadron in Alaska we were very mission-oriented and the schedule changed from day to day depending on what needed to be done to support the various bases and remote sites in our area. Laughlin AFB is a pilot training base. I settled into working a basic schedule on trainer jets. My first years of experience were spent working on large cargo planes and I had also worked on rescue helicopters while in Alaska. Working on trainer jets was entirely different, and the 100+ degree flight line was miserable; give me the subzero temps and a down parka any day! I had started to seriously reconsider if I would make the Air Force a career.

One deciding factor was to go back to school. I did exactly that, continuing with college classes, and applied for Non Commissioned Officer School. I was accepted, and I made NCO status below the grade and was put in a supervisory position. This enabled me to be inside the shop more often and not out on the hot flight line as much. My off-duty times were spent partying with friends, and I had drifted as far away from God as ever. My long-distance relationship had completely ended, as my romantic interest from Alaska had reconnected with an old girlfriend from home who he would later marry. I was as wild and free as my long hair.

I also moved off base into a single-wide, roach- infested motor home. At 25 years old I just didn't want to share a tiny dorm room with a 19 year old whom I had nothing in common with. I was counting the days until I could apply for a change in duty station. Before long, however, one of my coworkers who was a civil service employee told me about a friend of his who had recently lost his wife to cancer. My coworker wanted me to meet his friend and ask him for a date. When I asked details, I didn't follow through; he just seemed too old for me (he was 38).

Just a couple weeks later on Thanksgiving, I spent the holiday with this coworker and his family along with several others from our shop at work. Lo and behold, his widowed friend was also there for Thanksgiving dinner! We spent the entire day talking. I discovered that though I still thought he was too old for me, he was a very charming and nice guy. His wife had just died a month earlier after a long bout with cancer, and our matchmaking friends had things worked out perfectly.

He didn't ask me out though, so I did eventually ask him out for that first date. He seemed pretty nervous; you see, he had been married for 18 years to his high school sweetheart and hadn't dated in a very long time. So nervous, in fact, that he brought along our friend's wife on the first date! It was an interesting evening, and things moved along much faster than I had ever anticipated.

Just like my quickly growing hair, the relationship moved quickly, too. Within a few months I was easily talked into moving out of my roach-infested motor home and into his large home. A few months after that I had a beautiful engagement ring on my hand and started planning a wedding. As I look back at my diaries now I see that I was in great turmoil. Part of me had never expected to get married, another part had dreamed of an Air Force career, and yet another part vividly remembered the depression I felt when I arrived in Del Rio. Now here I was accepting a marriage proposal from a man who had no intention of ever leaving that town. All of this was poured out in words on paper, and interestingly I was praying more and crying out to God. But I didn't share that with anyone. Even my family got on the bandwagon, and everyone was so excited about the upcoming wedding. I was in love, and as my husband-to-be laughingly pointed out, "you aren't getting any younger". So we set the date and finalized the plans. I was honorably discharged from the Air Force after turning down a large reenlistment bonus, and I was suddenly wondering what would come next.

Jeremiah 29:4-7 This is what the Lord Almighty, the God of Israel, says to all those I carried into exile from Jerusalem to Babylon: "Build houses and settle down; plant gardens and eat what they produce. Marry and have sons and daughters; find wives for your sons and give your daughters in marriage, so that they too may have sons and daughters. Increase in number there; do not decrease. Also, seek the peace and prosperity of the city to which I have carried you into exile. Pray to the Lord for it, because if it prospers, you too will prosper."

1. How do you react when life goes in a completely different direction than you had always imagined?

2. How would your decision making be different if you presented everything to God first?

3. What does being in exile mean to you?

12

The Wedding

Picture it: a flowing gauzy gown, a wreath of flowers in waist-long hair, and an outdoor setting with a flower- covered arch under beautiful trees. That had been my lifelong dream for my wedding day (on those days when I actually imagined that I would marry). Now the reality: a rainy day in November, a very traditional white gown and veil with hair cut super short, befitting a 26 year old about to marry a banker. The ceremony was beautiful, held in the tiny Methodist church that I grew up in and had spent many wonderful times as a child. We were surrounded with friends and family and it truly was a great day, just nothing like I had ever planned for myself.

But, just like my very short haircut, this was the first inkling that I was allowing others to have control over my life. The wedding had been in the planning stages for about six months. My mother and sister, who both still lived in California, took charge of all of the details. They had get-togethers with friends to make the guest favors, they planned the menu (which was deliciously prepared by friends of my mother – a true hometown feast at the reception), and all I really did was show up a week before to step into the precisely planned events. I was not very good at saying no or voicing my opinion in those days, at least not to family members. To some extent, I wasn't even very good at it with my soon-to-be husband. Here is an example: he had been married for 18 years to his first wife, and they had worked hard to build a home for themselves. I moved into his first wife's dream home, which she only got to live in for a short time after it was built before she died. I even picked out dishes for my wedding to match the décor of the kitchen, never thinking that I could change that décor to suit me. Many decisions were made in just that way, and it has taken me a long time to realize that I don't have to just 'go along' so that others will be happy. In the long run, I make people more unhappy by being miserable to be around because of my discontentedness.

I look back at our wedding pictures, all of these thirty-plus years later, and wonder "who is that?" Why I let others' voices guide me to wear my hair a certain way and pick a gown to suit them rather than myself on my big day is puzzling. It is a day filled with wonderful memories, but it is also like looking back at someone else, someone who doesn't even resemble the real me. That was the beginning of when I felt like I was losing myself.

Ecclesiastes 4:12 Though one may be overpowered, two can defend themselves. A cord of three strands is not quickly broken.

1. God is the third strand in our marriage, though it wasn't always so. Where is God in

your relationships? Is He a third strand or just an adornment?

2. How do you express yourself to others in things that matter to you?

3. What is your decision making process when making life choices? Are prayer and seeking God's will part of that process?

13

The New Beginning

Starting this new phase of life, I was married! I was 26 years old, taking care of a house, no job and really didn't know what was coming next. That first year of being Mrs. Waylon Cowan was interesting! It was also reflected in my hair. From growing out that severe short haircut from before the wedding, highlights, different styles, and perms, it seemed I was as confused on my hair choices as I was in life.

One of the first things I did was get a real estate license. I love school, so the classroom portion of that was rather enjoyable. But after completing that course, selling one house and discovering that really wasn't for me, I was searching again. Things were going along ok; we had good friends, did lots of partying and generally I was enjoying life. Then came a big speed bump! Just 10 months after our wedding, as I was sitting in the doctor's office for my annual female checkup, the nurse told me the doctor wanted to order some more tests. An ultrasound was scheduled for that same day. I had suffered through menstrual issues since first starting that journey when I was 9 years old. Way too young! I called my husband and told him there was something wrong, and he got in the car and drove the three hours to San Antonio where I was having the exam done. We then sat in the doctor's office and heard that I had a golf-ball sized growth and extensive endometriosis. I asked about children, and he said that even if he did 'repair' surgery it was doubtful that I would ever conceive. As Waylon sat there and heard 'growth' all that went through his mind was burying his first wife about two years prior, and his response to my doctor was, "take it out, take it all out!"

I did ask if I could get a second opinion and I did that with my general practitioner. I went back to my gynecologist two weeks later and the growth had gone from golf-ball sized to grapefruit sized in those two weeks! The rapid growth was fueled of course by out-of-balance hormones. Though the growth itself was not cancerous, there were precancerous cells in the surrounding tissues. At the age of 27, I had a complete hysterectomy and started the process of accepting that I would never have a child. Though I really hadn't thought about it much, I never thought I would have to make that decision so suddenly and finally. I spent Waylon's 40th birthday recovering in the hospital, then my sister took me home to start the process of discovering who the new me was. No change in hair style could prepare me for the years ahead.

Isaiah 54:1 "Sing, O barren woman, you who never bore a child; burst into song, shout for joy, you who were never in labor; because more are the children of the desolate woman than of her who has a husband,' says the Lord.

1. When in your life have you faced a life-altering, unexpected event? How did you respond?

2. How do you respond when unexpected negative events happen in your life? What do you do, or could you do, to turn the negative into a positive?

3. What do you turn to in times of depression?

14

The "New" Me

Going through the hysterectomy and recovery was one of the hardest things I had ever experienced. I suffered through immediate hot flashes and other menopausal symptoms almost before the anesthesia wore off. I worked with my doctor over the next months, and eventually years, on coming up with a hormone replacement plan, none of which relieved my symptoms. In addition to that I also gained an enormous amount of weight, very quickly. Soon I was over 50 lbs heavier! From one who had always been slim and could basically eat whatever I wanted, to now be an obese young woman was devastating. I was no longer the cute, young banker's wife; I was now a matronly looking, overweight and unhappy twenty-something. (I remained overweight, fluctuating up and down for the next twenty plus years – more on that later).

Though I had never thought much about having kids, to have that decision taken from me so quickly was bringing on many emotions that I had to figure out how to deal with. At first I told myself that it didn't matter; Waylon and I had never really talked about children, so I just figured we would go along as we were. I soon found that I was searching for something, but I didn't know what. I also went through a time of change in my appearance. Learning to wear plus-sized clothes, wearing my hair longer again because I thought big 80's hair would offset my ballooning body. I also have always loved hats, but I quit wearing hats of any kind because hats draw attention and I didn't need any more attention drawn my way. Along with the big hair, more big changes were coming! My sister and her family had moved to Texas after she married Waylon's best friend. Soon after that our Mom also retired from her job in California, and she too moved to Texas to be near her two girls. Our lives began to be a whirlwind of fun family times, especially for these two California small-town girls married to good ol' southern boys! We had big hair, big dreams and lots of fun. Hidden inside of it all, for me, was a deepening sadness of many things lost forever. The dreams of a military career, the nomadic hippy life that I imagined after retiring from the military and then the fact that I wouldn't have children, ever. What would my 'old age' be like? So far my childhood dreams had all not come true, so I was getting to a place in my heart that the future would just 'be'. I certainly wasn't going to dream anymore! I hid behind my disappointments well; though my husband and sister knew my sadness, no one really knew just how dark my heart had become. Though I had always been good at hiding my deep relationship with God, I was missing the point entirely about how sharing our faith is what makes it grow. Now I was having a hard time praying anymore. My journal entries, that previously had been my way of pouring out my joys and concerns to God, simply became long rambling entries of how very depressed I was. I had forgotten how to pray.

Romans 8:26-27 In the same way, the Spirit helps us in our weakness. We do not know what we ought to pray for, but the Spirit himself intercedes for us with groans that words cannot express. And he who searches our hearts knows the mind of the Spirit, because the Spirit intercedes for the saints in accordance with God's will.

1. Recall a time in your life when God has seemed the furthest from you. How did you cope with that?

2. Take some time to reflect and journal about how you handle difficult situations.

3. Now consider how you respond to those closest to you when they are having hard times. Do you recognize when someone you love

is floundering? How could you be more aware of how others may be in trouble? Put yourself in their situation. How would you like them to respond to you?

15

And Then There Were Three

Several years kind of flew by. From 1984-1987 Waylon and I settled into a pattern. After I 'recovered' from the hysterectomy I just started to accept my life situation. I would never be thin again, no matter how many diets I tried. I would live in a town I hated, forever, because my husband loved his job and would not consider moving. I tried several things to occupy my time and finally found something I could be in control of, and actually enjoyed. We purchased a vending machine business and it was all mine! I had over 100 candy and coffee vending machines, located all across our community. It was an established business, and we bought it as-is from some friends of ours. The one employee came along with the ownership change, and Ernie drove the delivery van, keeping the machines full. Included in this business was a contract with the Air Force base for all of their vending machines, so I had a connection with the base again. I utilized my Air Force training in reading electrical schematics and I became not only the business owner but I did repairs on the machines, soon discovering that working on vending machine with jammed coins wasn't near as exciting as working on C130 cargo aircraft in Alaska! I was also in charge of product ordering, inventory management and all aspects of running the business. It came time for the contract with the base to renew, so I went through the process of bidding (and winning) to keep my machines on the base. It was nice to have a purpose again, though not anything like I had imagined.

In the summer of 1987 one of our couple friends had become pregnant (most of our friends were Waylon's age and they had all raised their children already – so we really had no friends that were peers of my age, other than this one couple). Being around them made me think about having a child. I had never really known anyone that adopted but I secretly started researching. I didn't tell anyone, not even my husband, what I was thinking. When I finally did I already had agency contacts, knew the process to go through an attorney and much more. When I decided to bring it up to him he kind of looked at me like I had lost my mind! By this time I was 30 and he was about to turn 43. After much discussion he finally said, "Let's do it." We had already been researching when we decided to tell our families; they were all shocked.

Then the heartaches returned. At first most agencies I contacted wouldn't even talk to us because he was over 40. We finally got an interview with a social worker at one agency and, during the interview, when they asked about him being married before, we were told they couldn't work with us because it was a second marriage. There was no consideration that his first marriage ended because she died of cancer! I cried and cried, again, because I could imagine never getting a child.

We did look into a private adoption, through an attorney, but the extreme high cost and all of the hoops to jump through were just too much. We had been telling everyone we knew about our search, and one day a friend told us of a new adoption agency opening in a nearby city. It had previously been a group working with women after abortion, but the founder was strongly convicted by God and moved in the direction of working with young women on adoption instead of abortion. I called this new agency and found out that the lead social worker had over 20 years experience in adoption placement, so though this agency was new she certainly had a long, successful career in working with families. Most of the other agencies also had years long waiting lists to even get an interview. Since Waylon was over 40 and I was 30 we didn't feel we could wait. It was the first time in a long time that I felt God moving in my life again. When I called the new agency we got an appointment right away, and we were placed in the next group of parents that they would be working with on placements. We had to drive the 3 hours to San Antonio for the group sessions, we were the oldest in the group and we were also the only ones who were unable to have children because of hysterectomy. All of the others battled different forms of infertility. I think the most heartbreaking was a couple that had conceived and lost several babies, the latest being a set of twins that were stillborn. They simply couldn't handle that grief again so they decided to adopt. In some ways I felt alone in my situation, because there was never any hope that I could conceive. These other couples still battled the emotions of going through adoption when *just maybe* they could still have a child of their own.

The main thing I noticed in that process was how great the trainings were. I have often thought that all couples should go through a training like that, to discuss parenting styles and decisions before children – not just those adopting. If more couples were required to actually talk through how they would handle life situations before they brought a child into the mix, I imagine much heartbreak could be avoided, or at least lessened. We were told that the agency was currently working with 13 young women, and there were nine couples in the group. Even if some of the mothers changed their minds, the social worker was pretty certain we all would get a baby. We finished the group sessions in February, had our home visit around Valentine's Day 1988 then received a call that we were fully approved as an adoptive family. All we had to do was wait. We knew the young women (and by this time more had come to the agency for prenatal care) would be delivering their babies at various times over the next few months. There was no set time frame; all of us in the group were approved at the same time. But we all had profiles of what we were looking for in our child. Some agreed to multi-racial babies, others with special needs, still others specified a certain gender! When we first filled out our form we were told in no uncertain terms "if you put such restrictive guidelines on your wishes you may never get a baby". So we loosened up on our desire that there be no substance abuse.

I set about getting the nursery ready, since we had the full go-ahead. My friends threw me a baby shower and I had clothes and items ready and waiting, all in green and yellow since we had no idea what gender our baby would be. Over what seemed like months of disappointment, and years of sadness, at the end of March I was sitting in Waylon's office at work when he got a phone call. We had a baby girl! There were many twists and turns in our adoption journey, including a fleeting moment when we were offered 2 year old twin girls to adopt, but decided against that. Then there were all of the turndowns from other agencies. This call was no different.

94

It came on March 25 - describing a baby girl born and placed in an affiliate agency in Tulsa. We got the call on a Friday. Since she had to come from Tulsa to Texas, we had several days to wait for all of the appropriate paperwork to be handled. We had a fun weekend alone in the Hill Country - (actually the town where many years later we would move) and on Monday the 28th of March we were waiting to hear from the social worker about the placement process. We did get that phone call, but it was nothing like we expected. She started the call with "I have never made a mistake like this in my entire career. We had a mix-up in paperwork and the baby I told you about on Friday is not available yet. We didn't have full release on that baby. *But* another baby girl was born today, also in Tulsa. She is healthy and both of her birth parents were present at the birth. Papers have been signed and she is yours!" So, while we didn't get the first baby she called us about, we did have a daughter. For just a moment I thought it was all crashing in on me again - the disappointment, the dashed hopes. But God had a plan. And when I looked back at my journals, the most amazing fact emerged: 9 months to the day of when I first wrote about adoption and made the first call to the first agency - we got the call that Chelsea Lee Cowan was ours. Nine months of disappointments, excitement, planning and surprises and the girl whom God had chosen for us was coming home.

Romans 15:13 May the God of hope fill you with all joy and peace as you trust in him, so that you may overflow with hope by the power of the Holy Spirit.

1. When has a time of hope come to you when you least expected it?

2. In looking back over your life, how has God been at work when you thought He had forgotten

you? What can you give thanks to God for when you remember difficulties that you have gone through?

3. When is it hardest for you to trust God? What is a way you could open yourself up to His joy, even in the midst of disappointment?

16

The Old Gray Mare - The Power of Words

I'm going to skip ahead a few years in my story. We had several events happen in those early years after adopting Chelsea; one gave me great excitement and hope. Waylon applied and interviewed for a bank president job in a town very near his hometown in central Texas. I was ecstatic! It was the first time he even remotely considered moving away from the border where we were living, in Del Rio, Texas. The day we went for the interview we even looked at homes and, one that was out in the country - complete with a horse barn and sitting on a hill - was calling to me. The process went on and he even was offered the job. He turned it down. The board wouldn't give him exactly what he wanted in regards to some benefits for employees, so he walked away from the opportunity to be a bank president and live in a small country town and a nice

salary.   I   was   completely   and   utterly
devastated.

I didn't say much for a long time. I
simply retreated into my depression and Waylon
went on about his work, playing golf, playing
cards with friends and our lives kind of went
in different directions. I immersed myself in
church activities and spiritually had a great
network   of   friends.   They   weren't   couple
friends, but they were my 'mommy' friends. I
survived.

One day in 1992, when Chelsea was 4 years
old, the time was right to make a move as far
as buying a house was concerned. Waylon knew
the home we lived in wasn't my ideal home,
though it was a beautiful house - it was his
first wife's dream home, not mine. I started
looking around town and found a wonderful
house that was built in 1924. It was nicely
restored and was located in the historic
section of town. With the huge pecan trees
and a spring fed creek running behind the
house it didn't seem so much like living in

the hot dessert. He still couldn't believe I wanted to leave a custom-built, fairly new home for an old, drafty one. When he agreed to put an offer on the house I really couldn't believe it! The next step was to sell ours, and that all fell into place too. On October 31, 1992 we moved into the house we would call home for the next 14 years. I loved that house! The charm of the rooms, the *feel* of the rooms, everything about the house made me smile (except maybe the utility bills). We did a lot of remodeling, restoring the modernized kitchen back to a style fitting of the lovely home. We removed years of carpet and vinyl flooring and had the beautiful wood floors shown off again. It was a labor of love that I did most of myself. I got things like miter saws and power tools for gifts to help me work on house projects. Working on that home kept me sane in many ways.

Our daughter was exhibiting more and more behavior problems, even as early as age 4. We had a lot of doctor care, learning some of her

100

chemical imbalance was probably a result of the substance abuse by her birth parents. Sometimes driving nails, tearing up flooring and painting walls and cabinets helped me retreat into my mind and heart for just a few hours each day.

One thing that was a routine for us during all of those years Waylon worked at the bank was he came home for lunch nearly every day. I often had his lunch prepared and would sit with him while he ate. We also have a pretty 'teasing' relationship and both like to give and take in the spirit of fun. One day I had been working really hard on the kitchen remodel; Chelsea was in elementary school by this time and I had my hair piled up on top of my head. When I walked out our side door with him at the end of lunch and was standing on the little porch, kind of tired from climbing up and down a ladder working on cabinets, he leaned out of his car window and said, "The old gray mare ain't what she used to be!" You see, I had started to have a few streaks of gray appear in my hair, and in the noon sunlight they were shining brightly when he decided to make that remark. I jokingly made a smart remark back as he had been gray from mid 30s and when I met him. As I went back to work in the kitchen, my mother's voice started to ring in my ears again: "You are too old for long hair". "Why don't you use a rinse on your hair, you have very nice hair; why look old with that gray hair?" My hair was shoulder length at that time and I loved it – but now he called me the ol' gray mare!? Not long after that remark, I went and had highlights put in my hair for the first time. I never liked having any color done on my hair, because it grows so fast and roots are not pretty!

Obviously that comment has stayed with me because all of these many years later I can still recall that scene vividly. Though I know he was teasing, for many years I carried the comment as a putdown and statement that I wasn't the cute, thin 26 year old woman he married. I have revisited that scene many times over the years and wonder if I had addressed it then would I be writing this very book all of these years later? I continued to lose myself.

Proverbs 16:24 Kind words are like honey – sweet to the soul and healthy for the body.

1. Recall a time when words spoken to you carried hurt or disappointment. How did you react?

2. Now recall a time when words you have spoken may have wounded another. Were you aware of the impact your words had?

3. Over the next few days, take notice of people around you and how they speak to each other. Especially those you love and are with the majority of the time. Do you speak words of kindness and love? Do you model kind words for those you have influence over?

* I will admit to you, this is a constant struggle of mine. Though I am often hurt deeply by things people say, I struggle to speak words of kindness. As I write this challenge I will be working on this with you! Each person that reads this chapter and these questions, I hope you will send me a message or email and ask how I'm doing!

17

The Middle

I don't want you to have the impression that my life was a depressing, endless stream of disappointments. Though I had deep desires I doubted would ever be met, our family had wonderful times over the years. Our daughter was active in dance classes, church and school activities. I spent lots of time in volunteer church ministry and loved every minute of it. Though Waylon and I led pretty separate lives, we also got together with his golf buddies and their wives, and we often traveled to be with my sister and her family for every holiday and vacation. Many great memories were made over the years.

When our daughter was 6 years old, a great opportunity came along for me that was a gift from God. She was in elementary school now and I didn't have a full-time job (I did dabble in seamstress work at home, and participated in a craft coop). One day I got a call from the pastor at our church. He told me they were creating a new staff position and thought of me. The position was for a Youth and Family Minister. I was so surprised and intrigued! I told Waylon about it and I shared with my two closest friends the desire I had to pursue this job. It was to be a part-time position, I could work office hours while Chelsea was in school and I would be in charge of the youth group activities each Sunday afternoon. There would also be ministry opportunities throughout the year, different things to participate in at different times. I applied, interviewed with the committee and was hired!

I had never done youth ministry, only children's ministry, but I quickly fell in love with it. To hang out with junior high and high school students, teach them about Jesus and attend the special events in their lives was a dream job. I started studying and attending workshops to learn all that I could. I formed relationships with those teens and their families, many of which are still my dearest friends even all these years later. Those 'middle years' when Chelsea was still young, Waylon was busy with his life and I had found my calling. I call them middle because they were the in-between time and a transition for me. I had moved from stay-at-home mom into a time of fulfillment and purpose for myself. Though I didn't know it was 'the middle' when I was in it, looking back now I do. Over those years I could also describe them like my hair: sometimes wild, sometimes 'styled', straight (going along as expected), permed (all twisted up as family and ministry life can be!) I was one who always wore my hair differently, and my life was the same – never the same, always changing with my moods. The lessons I learned from those teens, as I met with them each week and got involved in their lives, changed me forever. I started to go a little grayer, I started to share more of the 'me' that was inside and I can say I was content in 'the middle'.

Philippians 4:11-13 Not that I was ever in need, for I have learned how to be content with whatever I have. I know how to live on almost nothing or with everything. I have learned the secret of living in every situation, whether it is with a full stomach or empty, with plenty or little. For I can do everything through Christ, who gives me strength.

1. Has there been a time in your life when things just seemed to be going along well, no matter what your circumstances? A sense of *blessing* that blanketed you? To what do you attribute that feeling of blessing?

2. Recall a time when you felt you were functioning in a 'calling' – a feeling that you were at your best and things came naturally to you. What caused that time to be? How did you find yourself in that position or time period? Did you recognize it as a

108

calling, and how did you grow during that time?

3. Now think about people that were in your life during that time. What kind of relationships were formed and how did the people from that time have an impact in your life, and you in theirs? Do you still have contact with any of them?

4. How could you use what you learned from that time in your life now to help you when times aren't so smooth? Make an entry in your journal about how you listen for your calling and how or if you act on it.

18

Forty, Fishing and a Leap of Faith

1997 started out to be a fantastic year. I turned 40 in March of that year and celebrated on a Sunday afternoon with all of my youth group wearing black and throwing me a party. I didn't mind turning that age at all. I loved my ministry job, life at home was pretty good and Chelsea was healthy and happy.

Then even more great things came my way. I was offered a youth leadership position in our church district – it was a volunteer position, but I would be a liaison of sorts for all of the youth ministers in our west Texas district for our church denomination. I would be involved in planning district-wide youth events and helping lead and mentor other youth directors. I was so excited about this growth opportunity! I accepted the appointment without hesitation. The notice came in early summer and my duties would actually start in the fall, as youth activities geared back up after the summer break.

About the only thing that was a little sad spot in my life was the fact that Waylon didn't attend worship with us. He was very supportive of my ministry job, and always encouraged Chelsea to attend church with me (and she loved our church family). He just made it very clear that he had 'been there, done that' and it just wasn't for him. Waylon had been raised in a devout Christian home, but somewhat rebelled against the legalism. He also was, by his own admission, mad at God after the loss of his faithful Christian mom, who died at the early age of 42, and then also his first wife at the age of 36. He never could quite accept a loving God that would take the two most important women in his life so young. I regularly prayed for him, and my small group of praying friends also prayed regularly, that Waylon would discover the loving and grace-filled God that we knew and start to walk with Him.

Summer was a relaxed time for youth ministry, and it was a time we were able to take a nice family vacation. Our vacations were nearly always spent with my sister and her husband, who happened to also be Waylon's best friend. All of our holidays and vacations were usually spent together doing something as a family, mostly just hanging out at their small little country farm (second home). In 1997 we decided to do something very different. We arranged for our kids to be cared for and we went to east Texas to fish. We stayed in a small cabin at Toledo Bend Reservoir. We had several days of relaxation, lots of fun fishing and a little too much partying. But boy did we have fun!

We drove back to my sister's home in The Woodlands, Texas, to spend the night before the long drive back to our home. Our car was packed, complete with a large cooler of filleted fish all iced down for our long drive back to Del Rio. Since it was such a long drive, we planned to leave very early on that

112

Friday morning; and since I did all of the driving, Waylon was just getting ready to load up and go. Things changed very fast, and altered everything about our lives.

Waylon seemed to be running into walls, and his balance was a bit off. He also seemed a bit confused and had a headache. He tried to attribute it to a little too much to drink the night before. After our days fishing together, we had split up and the guys went out for steak and my sister and I went out for Italian on our last night together. When Waylon continued to miss doorways and stumble we knew something was very wrong.

Fast forward over the next few hours: Waylon was having a bleeding stroke at the age of 52. We knew he had vascular disease, as he had had a heart attack in his 30s, and he regularly had monitoring of his artery blockages and heart condition. When we learned it was a bleeding stroke in his brain, we were shocked and scared. We spent the next several days at an excellent hospital in

Houston and he underwent brain surgery to repair the bleed. With some residual peripheral vision loss and depth perception problems, we were learning how to journey through the maze of anti-seizure meds, tracking his vision to see how much of it would return, and a new 'normal' for all of us. We spent about three weeks staying there at my sister's home, close to the doctors and hospital while friends at home took care of our home and sent needed items to me. Since we had only planned to be gone for a 5-day vacation that turned into nearly a month, it took a lot of help to handle the details.

In the midst of this ordeal, Waylon had to lay flat on his back as we waited for the surgery. The first responder had given him aspirin, because since he has blockage issues it was assumed that perhaps plaque had dislodged and caused the stroke. We had to wait for the aspirin and other medications to clear his system before they could operate. My brother-in-law took the opportunity, with a totally captive audience, to 'share the Gospel and Proverbs' according to Chuck! Waylon couldn't get up and leave, so all he could do was listen. Chuck and I would take turns spending the night at the hospital with Waylon so that someone would always be with him. The night before the surgery I went home to try and rest and be with Chelsea, and Chuck stayed. The next morning we all arrived at the hospital, including Chelsea, to see her daddy. Since they were having to work fairly deep in his brain, none of us really knew what to expect. Chelsea was 9 and very strong in her faith. The 'What Would Jesus Do' bracelets were very popular at that time, and when Chelsea walked into the room she climbed on the bed and took off her bracelet and handed it to her dad. She said "Daddy, I want you to know Jesus". He looked at her and at all of us - and the next words were the ones I had longed to hear - "No matter what happens today, I know I'm going to be ok. I know God loves me and I know I belong to him. I believe and accepted Jesus last night".

Though scared to death of what the next few hours would bring, I was singing inside that Waylon had made that life-changing decision.

The remainder of 1997 was even more challenging as just 4 months after Waylon suffered the stroke and brain surgery, he then had a second heart attack and quadruple bypass surgery. In recovering from that surgery he developed a severe respiratory infection, lost huge amounts of weigh and, because of the fluctuations in medications, on New Year's Eve he suffered 2 grand mal seizures! I thought for sure, as I sat in the ICU waiting room, that I had lost him this time. If not for God's presence in both of our lives we never would have survived that year.

Psalm 103:1-5 Let all that I am praise the Lord, with my whole heart, I will praise his holy name. Let all that I am praise the Lord,

116

may I never forget the good things he does for me. He forgives all my sins, and heals all my diseases. He redeems me from death and crowns me with love and tender mercies. He fills my life with good things. My youth is renewed like the eagle's!

1. How have you reacted to life-altering, unexpected events in your life? How was your faith challenged or strengthened during those times?

2. Does God play an important part in your life, and where do you place Him in relation to other aspects in your life?

3. Have you ever shared your faith with someone who is reluctant to listen? Has anyone ever shared with you, if *you* are the reluctant one? How do you respond in situations like that?

4. How could you better prepare yourself for difficult life events? What do you think could strengthen you spiritually?
Are you willing to do that?

Take some time to ponder these Scripture passages and journal about them.

The Romans Road
Romans 3:23 The reality of sin
Romans 6:23 The result of sin
Romans 5:8 Christ's payment for sin on the cross
Romans 10:9 The need to believe
Romans 10:13 Assurance of salvation

19

Be Careful What You Pray For

Life was certainly different after Waylon's stroke, heart attack and surgeries. Waylon spent hours working jigsaw puzzles, good for the brain, and we walked together several times a day. He mainly had depth perception problems and when he would reach for items, like a fork or glass, his grasp would be slightly off. Many spilled drinks and dropped utensils later, he adjusted. His vision returned with the exception of a small vision cut in the lower right quadrant (so don't sneak up on his right side!) He was not back to work for a couple of months, and it was about the same length of time before he was cleared to drive.

When we returned home he was ready to give church a try. We returned to my church, and everyone greeted us warmly and were certainly glad things had turned out so well. Waylon, however, just never quite fit in with that congregation. I had been praying for so long, "God, please, just reach his heart and if he will attend worship I will go where he wants". A dear friend and golf buddy of Waylon's invited us to their church. It was a small Bible church, not affiliated with any denomination. We agreed to go visit, and Waylon liked it. True to my promise to God, I made the move to change churches. I turned down the district youth position, I resigned my youth ministry job and, although I was extremely sad, we quickly got involved with the new church. We joined a Bible study with several other couples, and that group of friends became our accountability and prayer group for the next several years. We went from living our separate spiritual lives to now hosting a small group at our home once a week. My "middle" was over, and I was moving in a new direction that I wasn't sure of.

Chelsea was also growing and changing. After leaving her very familiar church family from childhood, we started down the road of living with a teen in our home. Her friends didn't attend our new church and she was also going through big changes in school. All through elementary school she had attended a private school, with chapel every morning. We all loved that school, and I had even gone to work there as a teacher's aide and preschool teacher for her last years of attending there. The school only went through fifth grade, but she had been there since age 4. We made the difficult decision to homeschool during the difficult middle school years.

During this same time, not only was I preparing lessons and teaching Chelsea, but I had gone back to school myself, determined to complete the college degree I had started during my Air Force years. I took full-semester loads for the next several years, so I functioned on very little sleep, but enjoyed every minute of it. My hair had grown a little grayer by this time, and was often pulled back in a ponytail since I had little time to fuss with my hair. I certainly didn't look like the well put together banker's wife! I often looked at that one streak of gray at my temple and first began to wonder if I was too old to be back in school. My love of learning won out, and I received my Bachelor of Ministry in Christian Administration at the age of 47.

Though we were now a couple on the same spiritual path, I found myself sinking into that depression again. I was losing myself, giving up what I wanted (youth ministry) in order to follow my husband. Though we had wonderful friends at our new church, and our small group meetings helped me stretch my spiritual trust, I was drifting once again and feeling like I had no purpose. Two of my closest friends, who also had been praying for their husbands, were so envious that Waylon was now attending worship with me. I pretty much lost touch with them because the one thing we had in common was gone, and they felt like a change in their husbands would never come. I missed my friends and the depth of prayers we had shared over the years. I now know that I could easily have continued those relationships. I was the one who pulled away.

During this time I was also experiencing some troubling hair loss. I would have handfuls of hair come out in the shower. I needed to clean my brush daily of the hair that had fallen out during brushing. I had still been battling the weight issue for all of those years and, although I took thyroid medication, it seemed to be getting worse. All I ever wanted was long pretty hair, and now even that was not happening. Add to that the fact that our daughter was starting to exhibit more personality issues. As she went through puberty we started to see addictive traits emerge in her. Her obsessive interest in boys (not just your normal early teen curiosity), the early days of online chat rooms, and a new group of friends we really knew nothing about. All of the stresses in my life just seemed to pile on and then fall all around me like my rapidly thinning hair. "God,

123

I prayed and served you faithfully, why are you allowing all of this to happen to me now?" I thought.

Another life change was on the horizon, and just like the previous ones it came out of nowhere- God was certainly at work!

John 14:1 (Jesus' words to the disciples)
Do not let your hearts be troubled. Trust in God; trust also in me.

1. Have you ever prayer faithfully for something and then when it came about you didn't respond as expected?

2. How do you react when things don't go your way? Do you blame others, God or yourself?

3. Do you have a faith group that you can share prayers with, and if so are you open and receptive to doing so? How could you strengthen that bond, or if you don't have one, how might you go about building a

relationship like that? Think of someone you could reach out to, someone who may be needing you as much as you need them. Call, write or visit them

20

To The Head of the Class!

We decided to give the public school a try when it was time for Chelsea to enter high school. Though she had excelled in the private elementary school, and also did very well in her homeschooling for middle school, she was ready to venture out. We had our apprehensions, especially with her emerging and progressive personality disorder. I was able to monitor her medication, and made sure she took it every day, but she was earning more freedoms and we were encouraging her to make decisions based on the values and example we had modeled in our family.

She only lasted about 2 weeks at the large ninth grade campus. She was accosted in the girl's bathroom, her homework was stolen and she was bullied and ridiculed from day one. There were not many options in our town, but there was a small (very small) Christian high school that many of our church members were involved with. They had served on the school board, had helped form the school several years before, and Chelsea was ready to give it a try. The private school structure she was so familiar with worked for her. She once again was excelling in school and making some new friends. Even a few of her classmates from elementary school were also attending this small high school.

A couple of weeks after she started there the administrator of the school gave me a call. She knew that I had done seamstress work in the past and also had participated in the craft coop so she asked if I would be willing to teach a home economics class for the students. I was surprised, but thrilled! Not exactly youth ministry, but it would be working with teens again and since it was a Christian school we were able to bring spirituality into our teaching without fear of reprimand. The school board and staff were also made up of people from various denominations and we all worked very hard to provide a solid, college prep environment free from doctrinal arguments. I accepted the teaching position.

Just a few months later, over the holiday break, the administrator informed me she intended to step down from her position because of family issues, and asked if I would be interested in the position! I couldn't believe it! My degree was in Christian Management, but I also loved working with teens; it was a match made by God. I stepped into that position and went about working with the school board and staff to improve the school and help it grow as a solid, quality education choice in our town. There were five private elementary schools but no private middle and high school options. Only the Catholic school offered classes through the eighth grade, and they often had a waiting list.

Over the next couple of years I pursued College Board approval for us to administer the PSAT and SAT tests at our campus. We were an affiliate member of The Association of Christian Schools International and were working through the process for full accreditation through that organization. I also applied for and obtained membership in TAPPS (Texas Association of Private and Parochial Schools), which is an academic organization similar to UIL in the public school. Our small school had students competing in speech, linguistics and performing arts. Though we only had 19 students (yes 19, for grades 9-12) we were growing and becoming a quality school. We implemented Advanced Placement courses in our academic lineup and our students were performing above average in all areas. I was loving my job once again. We also had a turnover in the school board with a brand new member who was also chosen as the president.

During this time, I participated in a small Bible study group of women that I met with every week for devotional time and prayer. They were a real blessing to me and we had a close bond and could, and did, share from our hearts. One particular day, and I remember it well because it was my birthday, I was a little late for our weekly study. I had my mid-year evaluation with the president of the school board. She was one of my biggest supporters and just a week before had told me how happy she was in the direction the school was taking. I met with her in my office that afternoon right after school and was shocked when the words that came from her mouth were, "If we don't have your resignation by tomorrow morning, you will be terminated!" How could I have gone from receiving high praises to being fired in less than 10 days! I left my office stunned and drove to meet my friends for study. They greeted me with a birthday cake and singing and quickly realized that something was very wrong. When I said, "I was just fired," they thought I was joking. It would take me an entire book to explain the ins and outs of that event, but I will just say that it all came down to money, an

130

anonymous donor and lying by an employee that caused this series of events. The emotional toll was great, I was at my lowest level ever and the school eventually closed down within a year when the 'bad seed' was revealed. Sadly, the teachers were a great group of women and men that had no idea what was happening. They tried to stand in support of me, but they too were lied to in the process. One teacher also resigned before the school year was out when she confronted the board with proof that the teachers were all in support of me, and when I wrote an open letter to each of them the letters were taken from the desk and never distributed. Again, records altered by the wayward employee. All she and the board president had driving them was the promise of big money, on the condition that I was removed.

The hardest part of the whole ordeal was the effect on Chelsea. She loved her school, her teachers and her classmates. She was as devastated as I was at the loss of my position, and when she returned to school the next day and the board president led chapel – telling the students, "Mrs. Cowan has resigned, the teachers wanted her gone, and she has let you down". Chelsea was crying and telling her friends and teachers that is not true, when the woman told her, "Dry up your crying, your mother is gone – get over it!" One of the teachers had to drive her home, and a friend had to drive Waylon to the school to get her car to keep him from storming the school and getting involved. I really won't go into any more detail than this; it happened and very few people know the real story. I lost a much loved job in the most difficult way possible. I stood on my integrity and if people asked I told them I was an open book, and they were welcome to examine or ask me anything about my time there. It took time, but many people eventually came to me and expressed their sorrow and disbelief at what had taken place. I quickly sunk into what I thought was the lowest place in my life.

Psalm 17:1-3 O Lord, hear my plea for justice. Listen to my cry for help. Pay attention to my prayer, for it comes from honest lips. Declare me innocent, for you see those who do right. You have tested my thoughts and examined my heart in the night. You have scrutinized me and found nothing wrong. I am determined not to sin in what I say.

1. Have you, or anyone close to you, ever been wrongly accused of something? How did you react?

2. What process do you go through to determine truth when you hear things said about others?

3. How do you respond to people you have trusted when they hurt you, especially if they are Christian brothers or sisters?

Forgiveness is the cornerstone of the Christian faith. It is also one of the hardest things to put into practice. I have to work every day on forgiveness, and it is getting easier simply because if God can forgive me, how can I withhold forgiveness from someone else? Many times the person you forgive may not even know why you are forgiving them!

Forgiveness is not forgetting, but as you get better at forgiving the forgetting gets easier as well. Ponder this: *"Not forgiving is like drinking rat poison and then waiting for the rat to die." - Anne Lamott* or this one: *"Forgiveness is unlocking the door to set someone free and realizing you were the prisoner." - Max Lucado*

21

Back to the Mountains – A New View

After the shock of unexpectedly losing my job, I spiraled into depression. I stayed very quiet about the entire ordeal. I had never experienced anything like that in my life. My work record to that point had been excellent, and I valued my integrity. To the casual observer things looked like they were going along pretty well. We still met with our small group of couples each week, we were involved in the life of our church and I stayed busy with Chelsea.

She ended up also leaving the school just a few days after I turned in that 'resignation', as the stand-in administrator failed her in a quarterly class because she missed a test on the day following my departure. Her entire nearly perfect transcript was sullied from that grade. We arranged to homeschool her for the final quarter, and several of her teachers completed her courses through tutoring so she could have credit. She met with them after hours, completing her physics course and advanced math. We enrolled her in the local junior college where she took dual credit courses to fulfill her graduation requirement, along with some early college credits.

Over the course of the next 6 months, I didn't quite know how to handle the loss of my job. I had worked so hard and thought that position would be filling my time for many years. Chelsea was facing her senior year in high school, and we arranged for her to attend Christian Liberty Academy. This is a distance learning high school: she was in essence 'home schooled' yet the total curriculum was sent to us and I simply monitored her progress, and she filled in with the local college classes. She would go on to graduate at a walk-across-the-stage event the following summer in Chicago, with a class of about 75 other home-schooled seniors.

Toward the end of summer in 2005 my weight had ballooned back up, my hair was falling out from stress and I didn't seem to have any drive for anything. I was back to hating the town I lived in and saw no way out. No job, no real purpose, and my best friend was preparing to move. One day my sister called me and wanted to make an offer.

She and her husband were involved in ministry with a Christian dude ranch in Colorado. They would be going there in September to help the ranch staff close up for the winter, but while they were there a women's conference would be going on and my sister wanted to see if I would attend. Waylon and I talked about it and we decided to go. It was still horribly hot in September in Texas, and I jumped at the chance to go to the mountains.

As soon as we landed and made the hour or so drive to Estes Park, I started to feel just a small lift. As we wound up the steep few miles from Estes Park toward Long's Peak and arrived at the entrance to Wind River Ranch, I knew this place was where I needed to be. Some people love to go to the ocean and sink their toes in warm sand to relax and recharge. While I too love to sit and watch waves crash on a shore or walk along a sandy beach, nothing speaks to my soul like the mountains. In mid-September it was cool, the beautiful Rocky Mountains were starting to burst with the changing colors of aspen trees and snow on top of the distant peak. I just wanted to go off by myself and sit.

I usually love women's conferences, and retreats, but this time I really just wanted to be alone. I knew none of those women and I thought my sister would be participating with me, but she was working around the ranch helping close up cabins and work in the kitchen. Waylon was with the men working in the barn and doing other odd jobs around the ranch. I did participate, but my fondest memory (and life- changing one) was sitting on the deck of one of the larger cabins. The

138

meeting room was in this cabin, but the large deck had a magnificent view of Long's Peak, and I could also look down at the very old barn and see the activity of the wranglers. Another of my loves, and major bucket list item, is to have a horse. During this same week, the wranglers took the women on a trail ride up and down through the mountain trails. My trusty horse Dollar was a great ride. It was not exactly galloping across a pasture as I had done with my best friend in high school, but pure joy to ride a great animal if only on a simple trail ride.

I was starting to heal just a bit. I can't tell you exactly, these 10-plus years later, what the topic of the conference was. I met about 15 other women during that week, and most of them all knew each other. They were kind, but I often found myself sitting on that deck alone just praying and crying out to God, "what next!?" On the day before we were to leave, I was sitting on the deck in the afternoon, watching clouds roll in and around

Long's Peak. Looking at the aspens shimmering in the fall wind, it was as if I heard God Himself speak to me. The date was September 23, 2005 (I have a note written in my Bible beside a circled passage, along with some pressed aspen leaves that I picked up that day). The notation that I wrote, "*Sitting on the deck at Wind River Ranch, a major God moment, He spoke to me. This is a turning point – my delight is in Him*". This is no exaggeration: my hair stood on end – every hair on the back of my neck and all along my arms was tingling. I didn't know what it meant, but I knew change was coming. I walked down below the deck and picked up a small branch of aspen leaves to press in my Bible to remind me of the moment God spoke to my soul in those Colorado mountains. I told no one about the encounter.

Psalm 37:4-7 Delight yourself in the Lord and he will give you the desires of your heart. Commit your way to the Lord; trust in him and he will do this: He will make your righteousness shine like the dawn, the justice of your cause like the noonday sun. Be still before the Lord and wait patiently for him; do not fret when men succeed in their ways, when they carry out their wicked schemes.

1. Recall a time when you have separated yourself from activity and listened for God. Is that hard for you? If you haven't done that, how could you work time for that into your life?

2. What places recharge your soul? Do you make time to do that regularly? If not, what do you need to change in order to do so?

3. What one thing would you like to hear God say to you?

Pray for the Holy Spirit to lead you to a place, to prepare you, to listen for God to speak words of life to you.

22

A New Road to Travel

We headed back to hot, dusty Del Rio, Texas. My insides were kicking and screaming as we drove down that mountain - I just wanted to stay. I wanted to be in an area that I loved the most, surrounded by trees, rocks, mountains, horses and the place where God spoke to me! As my husband, sister and brother-in-law chatted about the week, I sat silently in the back and my thoughts drifted to my years growing up in the Sierra Nevada Mountains, then the couple of years I lived in northern California and explored Mt. Lassen and other mountain trails. Then I thought about my two years in Alaska and the beauty of those mountains. All wonderful, soul-recharging times surrounded by mountains.

Life quickly settled into a routine again as we got back home. Waylon was back to his work routine at the bank. Chelsea was busy with her senior year studies and working as a

142

student teacher at the dance studio. I was involved at church and leading a small group of women in a lunchtime Bible study. This was an unusual group: they were some friends, some acquaintances and it was something I had never done. We met once a week at a local pizza parlor dining room and I led about 10 women in study. I had facilitated many studies before, but always in the church setting. I loved the energy of that group. Working women, all ages, taking time out of their day to share together, and for some it was their first time studying the Bible. I had spent so many years leading and teaching children and teens that to interact with adults was something new, and I loved it! At Christmas that year one of the ladies gave me a gift of a one-of-a-kind journal. This is written inside the front cover: *Dec. 2005 "Merry Christmas Connie! Thank you so much for all that you've done for our group. I'm so thankful that you have taken this calling to be our leader. May God bless you & yours during this Christmas season".*

I read those words often when I first got that gift. I love journals, but for some reason I didn't use that one right away. It is handmade paper, with a wonderful twig binding. So unique and so special.

Right after Christmas that year, I mentioned to Waylon that I really loved teaching those women and I wanted to think about doing something along those lines. There really were no job opportunities in Del Rio, so I started looking everywhere. I finally wrote the first entry in that special journal *on* February 1, 2006: *A journey – after receiving this handmade journal as a gift I knew I would need to record something special in it. I feel a journey has been in planning and it is evolving with each moment. Ever since arriving in Del Rio nearly 24 years ago I have wanted to leave. Even though some wonderful things have taken place here, in some ways defining who I am, I know in my soul I will be moving to a place other than Del Rio for the next phase of life. I don't know when, where or how, but I intend to record my thoughts prayers and 'hunches' about this journey here. Should be fun to see how it all unfolds!*

Just a week later I made an entry about a job that I found in Fredericksburg, Texas. It was for a full-time Christian Educator job at the Methodist Church! Though not the mountains, the Texas Hill Country was a favorite of ours; we often took little get-aways there and often dreamed (or at least I did) of moving there. When I told Waylon about the job, he said "go for it!" Chelsea was about to graduate from high school, and Waylon would be turning 62 that year. He talked to his accountant and we decided if everything fell into place he could retire early and we could move. I have never been so shocked in my life! Waylon had lived and worked in Del Rio at that bank for 35 years; he had often said he would never leave.

I took the first step and applied for the job. Much to my surprise, I got a call rather quickly for an interview. Over the next few weeks I made two trips to Fredericksburg, for two separate interviews. My little journal is full of my thoughts about the whole process, not really believing that it was happening. Then I remembered my encounter with God at Wind River Ranch and told myself to trust and delight in the Lord. My first focus was Him – everything else would fall into place.

I have notes of comments people made to me. I had been asking everyone I knew to pray with and for us as I pursued this job. Finally, in mid-April, I was called back for another interview and then offered the job. Just over a year after my worst birthday ever, when I was let go from a job I loved, I had a chance to walk a completely new path. I could not believe it! When Waylon and I talked and prayed about it, he said the magic words, "I think we can make it work." I accepted. I would start on June 1.

Psalm 63:7-8, 11 Because you are my helper, I sing for joy in the shadow of your wings. I cling to you; your strong right hand holds me securely….. but the king will rejoice in God. All who trust in him will praise him, while liars will be silenced.

1. When you look back at a time when you had to wait for something, how did you feel during the waiting?

2. Now that the waiting is over, how do you view the time period differently, and what thoughts come to mind as you reflect?

3. Has there been a time in your life when a seemingly bad event has turned out to be the catalyst or beginning of something better? How did you move through that time? If not you, how do you help those around you who may be experiencing a disappointing life change?

4. Write your thoughts or share with a friend or group about what trusting in God means to you.

22

New Hair - New Home

The next few weeks were a whirlwind of activity. Chelsea was finishing her senior year studies, and I signed a 6- month lease on an apartment. Waylon would finish out the year in Del Rio before retiring, get our house ready to sell and I would explore homes in the area. Chelsea came with me for the summer and stayed busy with the praise team at the church and various other activities before leaving for college.

Before moving I got a new, short haircut. I don't like short hair, but I was going to be working full time - with all new people - and over the course of that last year with my excess weight and depression I just kind of let everything go. So off I went with a short bob and wondered what the job would be like. Getting a new haircut or style change shocks me sometimes. When I was so very overweight, I rarely looked in the mirror. I didn't like what I saw, and I also avoided photos like the plague. It was as if I could ignore what I had become if I just didn't look at myself. Now here I was every day looking in the mirror, styling my hair and meeting new friends. I was loving every minute of it.

The first big shock was the progress on finding a home. The area in town is very expensive so I had been looking at homes in the country, outside of the city limits. We were limited in our budget, and though I dreamed of building a home I knew that wasn't going to happen. I was (and still am) somewhat of an HGTV junkie. I love watching those home improvement shows and what can be done with fixer-uppers. I had spent so much time on the old house in Del Rio; if I could have picked up that 80-year-old house and placed it in the hill country, it would have been perfect. That wasn't going to happen, so I spent all of my off hours driving around looking at homes for sale. I found one about 6 miles from town and sent pictures to Waylon.

He said he didn't think so, but told me to line up a viewing. The next time he came up, we went and looked. When we walked into the house, he looked at me and I could tell he was thinking, "have you lost your mind – again!?" You see, this house was so far from a style that I usually dreamed about. It was a 1979 ranch style, but every room was filled with massive antiques, all the walls were 1970's wood paneling and each of the three bedrooms was painted in varying shades of pink. The bathrooms were outdated, and the kitchen was a mess with the original indoor-outdoor carpet. About the only saving grace was it sat on 3 acres of mostly wooded land and had an area that could be used as a workshop. It also was within our budget.

As soon as we walked through, I told Waylon what we could do with it. We worked out a finance plan, since we hadn't sold our home in Del Rio yet, and we haggled and settled on the contract. We purchased our home in the country on June 30, just one month

151

after I arrived in town. On the first weekend, the 4th of July long weekend, Waylon and I alone took sledgehammers and completely gutted the kitchen and started on the major remodel. Just the two of us tore out all of the nasty carpet throughout the entire house. Waylon only made the 3 hour drive from Del Rio every other weekend, and I moved out to the house from the apartment in mid-July. There was no kitchen, and I had no furniture other than an easy chair, a TV and a rollaway bed. We had the new kitchen cabinets and appliances professionally installed and tile flooring installed throughout the home. I tackled the paneled walls. After working full days at my new ministry job, I spent nights and weekends doing a faux stucco finish on the walls - I was going for a Tuscan look, which I did achieve. The finishing touch was in the kitchen, where I had stenciled Psalm 37:4 - *"Delight yourself in the Lord and he will give you the desires of your heart"* - the verse that had come to me when God spoke on the

152

September day exactly one year before at Wind River Ranch.

Through this first 6 months in our new home, I often wore a bandana on my hair. It was a covering, to keep paint and plaster out of my hair and also to keep my hair from hanging in my face in the heat. I think of that bandana and the 'covering' that was taking place from God. Though we had moved to a place that I quickly fell in love with, some of the worst times in our lives were coming and I certainly needed to be covered!

Proverbs 27:1 Don't brag about tomorrow, since you don't know what the day will bring.

1. What is your relationship with God when things seem to all be going really well?

2. Do you spend as much time in prayer of gratitude as you do in prayers of "want" in times of need? Have you ever taken note of how

attentive to God you are in the positive times
of life?

Spend some time being grateful, acknowledging
the blessings in your life and thanking God
for them, especially the small ones.

23

The Darkest Cloud

Over the next 3 years some of the best things were happening in my life. We continued to work on our home remodel, we had a new small group of friends that we worshipped with, studied with and just had lots of fun with. I loved my job and one of the biggest blessings was I finally got my health in order. A doctor finally helped me get my 20-year battle with thyroid and hormone issues balanced, and I lost more than 65 pounds with Weight Watchers. I was the healthiest I had been since my early twenties and I had just passed the 50-year milestone birthday. I was blessed with so many good things in life.

At the same time some of the very worst things were happening as well. I will briefly give you a timeline, but won't go into great detail as that would take an entire book! All of these troubling events revolved around our daughter:

2006: Left for college, didn't manage her meds

2007: Withdrew from college, abusive relationship, back surgery for herniated discs, new college, new guy,

2008: Engagement, pregnancy, wedding, deep depression, moved in with us so she and her husband could find jobs

2009: Our first grandchild was born, more addictive habits, divorce, Chelsea and 6-month-old Chloe move in with us

We spent the next 18 months or so parenting our granddaughter and trying to help our daughter find her way back to herself. She moved in and out from our home and had various jobs and relationships. She sunk deep into depression, and we didn't know how to help.

2010: New guy, fast decisions

2011: Second marriage, move across the country with her Army husband, much grief and worry on our part about their future

2012: Second granddaughter born, they left the Army and returned home to move in with us until they found a home and jobs, troubled marriage and lots of worry

2015: Second divorce, finally putting her life together

So here I was, in 2007, finally living the life I had so long yearned for. We had moved away from the border, I had a great job and we had a spirit-filled, fun group of friends. I was healthier than I had ever been. All overshadowed by the angst of our daughter's life. I had a strong accountability partner and friend that would listen to me rant and rave and cry. She prayed with me, loved me and helped me see that my adult daughter needed to find her own way, that I could not be her rescuer.

In the midst of these years we also had a huge financial setback. Since Waylon had a nice retirement account, we spoke at length with a financial advisor about our options. We felt assured that our mortgage could be serviced from his IRA account, he could retire early at age 62 and, with my full-time salary, we could cover living expenses. Then 2008 hit. Many of you will remember that as a horrible financial time for our country, and it depleted a large portion of his retirement account. So, at age 64, Waylon went back to work as a part-time chaplain at the local hospital. He had done some chaplaincy work in Del Rio as a volunteer, and he had been leading the Stephen Ministry at our church, so it was a natural flow to work part time as a chaplain and bring in some needed money. We also were being depleted because we continued to help our daughter financially through each step of her troubled journey. Much like when I would get advice from well- meaning friends when she was a child, like, "You just don't discipline her enough," or "You are letting her walk all over you," we started to hear some of the same things during this time period: "You just need to turn her out, she is an adult and needs to learn!" "Until you make her do it on her own, she will walk all over you". What many people don't understand is we walked the path of mental health issues with Chelsea from the day we adopted her. Our society carries such a stigma about mental health, and invisible illness is often brushed off – with many people believing the person can just shake it off and they are just choosing to be in the state that they are. Even Waylon, at times, couldn't understand why Chelsea would make the decisions that she did. Clinical depression and personality disorders often don't respond to medications like other conditions. I studied and researched at length in order to understand and try to help the daughter I love so much.

In the summer of 2010 things just piled on a little too much, and I started to break. My mom died after a long battle with Parkinson's and dementia. Things were changing at the church, and the job I loved became a *job* more than a ministry. I was so depleted from our family issues that I had little to give to the children and adults in my education programs. I also took on more work as a Weight Watchers leader for two reasons: I wanted the accountability in order to keep that weight off that I had lost, and I loved working with adults and helping them improve their health. My best friend moved, our small group pretty much fell apart and I was wondering how things that had been so good, could suddenly turn so bad. The church also had been suffering in the economic downturn since 2008, and my position was being considered to go to part time. I found another program director job in town and I worked out a schedule to work each job for 20 hours a week and also continue to lead Weight Watchers meetings. I kept myself so busy that I had little time to do much else. In the summer of 2011 I left my dream job at the church completely and took a full-time position at the local historical museum.

Depression began, but I hid it well. My hair started falling out again…… I cried.

Psalm 25:16-17 Turn to me and have mercy, for I am alone and in deep distress. My problems go from bad to worse. Oh save me from them all!

1. What ways does your body tell you that it is in distress? How do you respond?

2. Who in your life is a safe haven for you, someone you can share deep thoughts with and trust them with your most intimate worries and prayers? If you have no one, what keeps you from fostering that type of relationship?

3. How do you handle situations when others come against you and your decisions? Do you consider God in the decision making?

Pray for a trusted friend to come into your life, someone who needs you as much as you need them!

24

The Second Big Chop

I started this hair journey with the first big chop when my mom took me to Bev's Beauty Shop for that pixie haircut. In the spring of 2012, I did it to myself. In 2011, our daughter had started her second marriage to a young man she had only known for a few months, most of which he spent away at Army basic training. She flew to watch him graduate and married him there. We spent a whirlwind month helping her get ready to move to Washington state, halfway across the country, and I cried buckets over our precious 2-year-old Chloe moving away. I played over every scenario in my head of what could happen. I was working at a job I really didn't like at the museum, mainly because of a narcissistic boss who had no respect for women. I did love my Weight Watchers job, though it was very part time. In May of 2012, our second granddaughter was born and I was preparing to fly to Washington to meet her and help out with 3-year-old Chloe. I decided to make a big change.

A new neighbor had moved in across the road from us and we struck up a friendship with her. She had relocated from California and opened her own hair salon. We often helped each other house sit, water plants, care for animals and such, so she offered to give me free haircuts in return for some work Waylon would often do at her home. My hair at this time was about mid-shoulder length and not in good condition because of my depressed state. Though I was still thin, I wasn't taking good care of my health. I would often hear my mom's voice in my head, especially in my dark moods, saying, "You are too old for long hair." So, I sat in that stylist's chair, covered in a plastic drape just like when I was 6 years old, and told my friend, "cut it off, cut it all off." She did just that! As she snipped I told her to go shorter, and I walked out of her salon that day with hair that was close to a boy-buzz, slightly longer and spiky on top. It was easy; I could rub it with a towel and put a little gel on it and was done. I got so many compliments, from, "you look so much younger!" to "that is the cutest haircut on you!" My friend got some new referrals to her salon because people loved my hair. I started on the much hated habit of frequent trims, as often as once a month because my hair grows really fast. In order to keep that carefree style it needed to be cut often. I hated it from the moment she turned me around in the mirror – but I kept that short hair style for a year. I was being a 'pleaser' again. Listening to my mom's voice and also remembering that day many years before when Waylon made the comment about the old gray mare when my first streak of gray appeared. I was losing me in the biggest way ever and really didn't know what to do.

Psalm 22:1-2 My God, my God, why have you abandoned me? Why are you so far away when I groan for help? Every day I call to you, my God, but you do not answer. Every night you hear my voice, but I find no relief.

1. Have you ever made drastic or split-second decisions in the midst of anger or depression? How did it make you feel?

2. Have you ever done something to punish yourself, thinking you deserved it?

3. How do you feel when people compliment or encourage you in things that are the opposite of what you want for yourself? Do you go along with them or their expectations for you? Do you consider what God wants for you?

Write a prayer for God to reveal to you what HE wants for you and how you should respond in decision making.

25

A Soul Baring Moment

The year 2012 was an up-and-down one. After the big chop, I flew to Washington to meet our new granddaughter Ryleigh Jayne. What a joy! In the midst of that, however, while spending 10 days with them in Army post housing, it was evident that things were not all love and roses. Warning flags were waving for me in how my son-in-law was treating Chloe. He is younger than Chelsea and to go right into a marriage, adopt a 3 year old and then have a baby in the first year of marriage is hard anyway; but they barely knew each other before they married so all of it was stressful. Also, it was hard being so far away, as we had always been very close to Chelsea. She was suffering again from postpartum depression, and I was proud of her for taking advantage of the medical services the Army offered to be under a doctor's care.

I flew back home and sank even deeper in depression.

Later in the year, they were unexpectedly discharged from the Army and moved back to Texas. So now we had a young couple with no jobs, a preschooler and a 6 month old all living in our home that was definitely not roomy enough for all of us. Before too long, we managed to co-sign and get them in an apartment of their own, which added to our financial woes. Our debt mounted, I was unhappy in my job and I was constantly worried about Chelsea and her children.

As 2012 came to an end, I knew I needed to make changes. I took a giant leap of faith and quit the museum program director job. Waylon was supportive of the decision, and we figured we could go 3 months on the money we had and cover our bills. By this time I was leading two Weight Watchers meetings a week, which provided very little income. I heard about a possible work-from-home job with Weight Watchers and I called my territory manager. Over the course of the next few months, I started doing scheduling and support work from home and was at least making a little more money.

One afternoon, in April of 2013, I was sitting in our living room, having just finished my online work when Waylon looked at me and asked, "What is bothering you?" I had been very quiet, and my moods are very readable in my body language. After almost 30 years of marriage he could tell something was very wrong. I blurted out, "I HATE MY HAIR!" I thought he was going to bust out laughing. He looked at me and just asked what in the world I was talking about. I then went on a long rambling course of words, with lots of tears mixed in and tried to explain that I hate short hair on me. It was as if my hair, in that super short haircut, was a reflection of everything I had become over the course of my adult life. I had made choices and missed opportunities and let others make decisions for me nearly all of my adult life. I had

169

molded myself into a person I thought everyone expected me to be, yet I had totally thrown away or smothered the person I wanted and believed God wanted me to be. It was, and still is, hard to put into words how it felt to be 56 years old and have no real career, not having accomplished many of the things I had dreamed of growing up and thinking that none of those things would ever come to be. I had left the military when I wanted to make it a career, I had let others plan my wedding and 'dress me up' the way it was expected of a banker's wife. I had neglected to take care of myself and spent the majority of my young adulthood overweight and letting medical conditions I couldn't control destroy parts of my body. Then the one thing that I love the most - long hair - I had cut off. It may seem trivial, but sitting there that day all of it crashed in on me and it came out as hating my hair. After my long crying and yelling discourse he quietly said, "So grow your hair." I looked at him and reminded him of his teasing comment all those years ago about the old gray mare, and he was shocked. He couldn't believe that I had carried that joking comment for so long and allowed it to fester in me, causing me to make decisions about my own appearance.

At this same time, things were still rocky with Chelsea. On top of that, my sister and her husband were doing quite well financially and our lives had become very different. They had purchased a large motor coach and were spending months traveling around the country. Judy and I would communicate daily via email; she has always been my most trusted confidant. She could tell from the tone of my emails for many months that I was in a severely depressed state. She tried to get me to go to the doctor, and she encouraged me to take meds if necessary. As one who is an advocate for mental health, I resisted any help for myself. Like many who suffer from depression, I thought I could pull myself out.

I hadn't been doing much Bible study since leaving my ministry job, and Judy suggested that we do a study together and share our responses with each other, since we were already writing each day anyway. She chose the first book, and we worked our way through the study. I rediscovered my love and dependence on prayer and looking to God for answers. I also shared with her my breakdown with Waylon and that I was going to grow my hair out long!

Doing the study with her had been a turning point for me, and I was hungry for God again. As we finished that study, I chose the next book. She agreed. It was interesting though; she really struggled with that second book and I was devouring it! It was a self-study about discovering your divine purpose, examining yourself to really look at who God created you to be. I loved it! It fell right in with my desire to quit being the person others expected me to be and live and thrive in who I was created by God to be. It was so freeing, and the growing of my hair has been the visible sign of my transformation. Through the course of the study there were exercises to formulate a vision or purpose statement of sorts. As I worked through the process I came up with this, my purpose – "communicate freedom". I love speaking and leading and sharing with people, particularly women. By communicating, and learning how to effectively do that, so much can be avoided. How different my life would have been if I had said to my mom "I don't want short hair and a traditional veil on my wedding day, I want long hair with flowers". I would probably love looking at my portraits instead of looking at them rarely and only seeing someone I don't recognize. Or all of the instances in my life when I held things in instead of communicating how I really felt or thought. The only person I was hurting in all of that was myself, and I was stifling the person that was inside of me. Freedom has come to me in communicating.

I'm still not great at it. I tend to bottle up feelings and emotions so that no one knows what is really going on. By listening to someone I love deeply and letting her prod me on through a difficult time, I started on a path to healing. I thank God for my sister Judy every day. Like my growing comfort in being me, my hair also started to grow. I loved it!

Proverbs 16:31 Gray hair is a crown of glory; it is gained by living a godly life.

1. **What outward signs do you display that are reflections of the real you?**

2. **Have you neglected yourself and your purpose in order to go along with what others expect of you? How does that make you feel?**

3. **Long hair is my expression of *me*. What would you say is your expression of *you*? What makes you feel free?**

4. Is there something in your life that you have avoided or suppressed because you feel it goes against the norm of society? How could you change that?

26

Discovering Me

I am nearly 3 years into this journey toward long gray hair. I started on that April afternoon in 2013 when I had the breakdown with my husband. I have had a few trims to even out the growth, but I have gone from about an inch long on top and multiple layers, to hair that now extends to the middle of my back. It is long, gray and healthy. God willing, I plan to let it grow as long as I can, with simple trims along the way.

Along with my hair, I have also embraced the total me. I wear clothes that I like and make me feel comfortable. I make time for myself, to be alone and communicate with God. I pursue hobbies that give me pleasure, and I work at a job I love. I started this book 2 years ago, and I came up with the title before I ever wrote the first word. I was leading a women's retreat and I shared with that group that I was writing a book and would have it ready for our next retreat. That was 2 years ago, and here I am just now finishing it. What I learned is that this book was a process too - I had much still to discover before I could complete it.

A year ago, I took another giant leap of faith. I had been working full time for Weight Watchers since late in 2012. I had full benefits and enjoyed the job. I led five meetings a week and worked from home as a territory manager assistant. I was feeling the deep stirrings of what I was to do next, and leading retreats, speaking and writing have always been simmering inside of me. In the summer of 2014, as our finances were still in much dwindled supply, I decided to join a direct sales company. I had tried some of those before, but this one seemed different and I loved the product. I jumped in with both feet and loved it from the beginning. I started to build a team of women across the country, and one of my biggest joys of the job is mentoring them and helping them discover the potential within themselves. Direct sales is hard; there is no guarantee of success. One has to be self-motivated and determined to work even when you receive repeated 'no' answers to your request for parties or sales. I kept on.

In the winter of 2015 I decided, after deep prayer, to completely quit my other jobs and focus only on my direct sales business. It was scary and a big step, but I have never regretted it. I am able to work from anywhere, and it also frees me up to pursue the things I feel I'm called to do: lead retreats, write this book and spend time with my family. The concern over money is always present, but I trust God in my decision.

As I am writing this, my 71- year-old husband continues to work so we can pay bills. We continue to help support our daughter, as she traveled through a second divorce a few months ago. She is in a good place right now, and her daughters now have a safe and happy home. We are blessed to be part of their everyday lives.

My journey to long gray hair is not over - yet it is a pleasant journey at the moment. There are often days of worry and wondering how we will get by and what the future holds. There are many sideways glances from strangers at the oddly dressed almost 60 year old with long hair and flowing, somewhat hippy, clothing. Certainly not the 'banker's wife' of my youth! I am comfortable in who I am, I am blessed to be God's child and I pray my story has encouraged you to discover yourself, no matter your age.

Genesis 1:27 So God created human beings in his own image. In the image of God he created them; male and female he created them.

1. How do you acknowledge the *you* that God created? How do you stifle His creation?

2. What have you learned about yourself in working through this journey with me?

3. What can you share with others about discovering themselves?

4. What is your biggest take-away from this book? Please write an entry to God about your discovery.

I welcome your comments about my humble journey and what it may have awakened in you. Please write to me and share your story with me!

Connie Sue Cowan

longgrayhair@gmail.com

For retreat speaking, please send an email with "retreat" in subject line.

For information about Wind River Ranch

    A Christian Family Dude Ranch

    Estes Park, CO   1-800-523-4212

    www.windriverranch.com

Memories of Wind River Ranch and my 'moment with God' 2005

The Big Chop

1975   2015

Party Girl - 1979

Elmendorf AFB, Christmas 1980

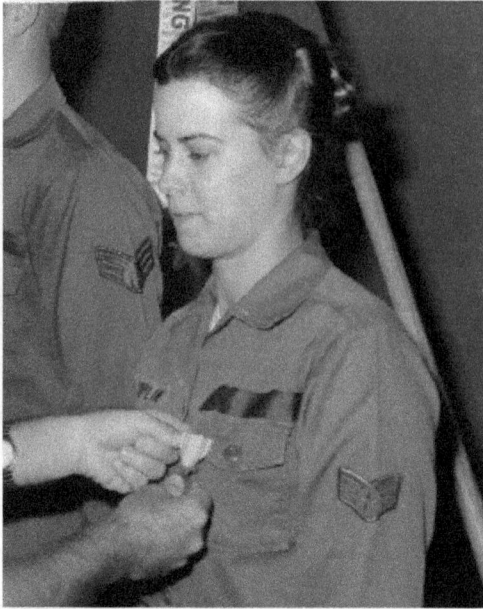
Senior Airman Koplin

Thanksgiving 1982- Day I met Waylon

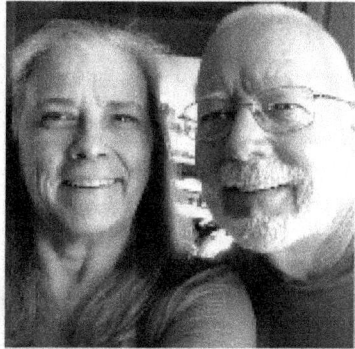

The Wedding Chop 1983, and 32 years later

Miniature horses and BIG me!

2005 – Judy and me (unhappy) on a sister outing

Big Chop #2 – with Chloe Grace

Christmas 2015 – my girls!

Chelsea, Ryleigh Jayne, Chloe Grace and me

.

189

www.ingramcontent.com/pod-product-compliance
Lightning Source LLC
Chambersburg PA
CBHW060924040426
42445CB00011B/779